KT-463-291

Urban Sprawl

ISSUES
(formerly Issues for the Nineties)

Volume 1

Editor

Craig Donnellan

Independence
WORCESTER COLLEGE
OF TECHNOLOGY

0097400

First published by Independence
PO Box 295
Cambridge CB1 3XP
England

© Craig Donnellan 2000

Copyright
This book is sold subject to the condition that it shall not,
by way of trade or otherwise, be lent, resold, hired out or otherwise
circulated in any form of binding or cover other than that in which it
is published without the publisher's prior consent.

Photocopy licence
The material in this book is protected by copyright. However, the
purchaser is free to make multiple copies of particular articles for instructional
purposes for immediate use within the purchasing institution.
Making copies of the entire book is not permitted.

British Library Cataloguing in Publication Data
Urban Sprawl – (Issues Series)
I. Donnellan, Craig II. Series
307.7'2

ISBN 1 86168 139 9

Printed in Great Britain
The Burlington Press
Cambridge

Typeset by
Claire Boyd

Cover
The illustration on the front cover is by
Pumpkin House.

CONTENTS

Introduction

Urban Sprawl is the first volume in the **Issues** series. The aim of this series is to offer up-to-date information about important issues in our world.

Urban Sprawl looks at Britain's housing problems.

The information comes from a wide variety of sources and includes:
Government reports and statistics
Newspaper reports and features
Magazine articles and surveys
Literature from lobby groups
and charitable organisations.

It is hoped that, as you read about the many aspects of the issues explored in this book, you will critically evaluate the information presented. It is important that you decide whether you are being presented with facts or opinions. Does the writer give a biased or an unbiased report? If an opinion is being expressed, do you agree with the writer?

Urban Sprawl offers a useful starting-point for those who need convenient access to information about the many issues involved. However, it is only a starting-point. At the back of the book is a list of organisations which you may want to contact for further information.

*****

Britain's housing problem explained

By Patrick Barkham

Why all the fuss about housing?
Post-war trends have seen the depopulation of city centres, particularly in the north, as people have sought jobs in the booming south-east or a better quality of life in the countryside.

With the fragmentation of traditional families, 80% of the demand for new housing will be for single people. However, the vast majority of houses built in the past 30 years have three or more bedrooms.

To meet demand, experts say, a huge number of new houses will have to be built in Britain, particularly in the south-east. Those living in small towns, rural communities and environmentalists fear that the countryside will be concreted over.

How many houses do we need?
Estimates differ. A report by Professor Stephen Crow for the government last autumn predicted that south-east England would need 1.1m new homes over the next 20 years to prevent escalating house prices, sluggish transport (as people travel further from where they live to work) and the shift of business to mainland Europe. In contrast, local planning authorities have proposed 718,000 new homes outside London over 20 years.

The government has set a target equivalent to 860,000 new homes over the same period. It favours a five-year plan initially, for 43,000 homes a year outside London in the south-east and 23,000 a year in the capital. Development outside London will be concentrated in the Thames estuary, Milton Keynes, Ashford and, potentially, the M11 corridor near Stansted.

Is Britain going to be buried in concrete?
Since the sprawling 'ribbon development' along roads at the start of the 20th century, alarmists have pre-dicted that soulless surburbia will swallow up what is left of Britain's countryside. It has not yet, but what is alarming about current development is that it wastes land.

'We insist on building as if we lived in the American midwest or the Australian outback,' says eminent architect Lord Richard Rogers, whose Urban Task Force reported to John Prescott, the secretary of state for the Department of Environment, Transport and the Regions last summer.

Over the past 10 years British builders have constructed 23 houses or flats per hectare of land, which is disastrously extravagant for a country of relatively little space. The US builds on average 40 dwellings for every hectare, as Britain's green 'garden city' movement at the turn of the 20th century recommended. This compares to 60-80 housing units in a traditional Cornish village, 100 houses per hectare in Georgian cities, 200 in Victorian ones, and 400 units in modern Barcelona.

Does high-density equal high-rise?
Increasing house density does not mean the return of high-rise blocks. Taking a firmer line on the size of executive homes and private garages and stopping developers building ornate brick driveways, for instance, could make for denser housing.

Lord Rogers believes that, well planned and built, high-density suburbs are a better use of land than the high-rise blocks, which leave too much wasted, windy space between them.

'High-density urban areas, if well managed and planned like the Georgian parts of our cities, are attractive to live in,' says Lord Rogers. Denser housing can reduce dependence on the car and create vibrant communities, encouraging 'civic pride, a sense of security and social and economic integration'.

What is the government going to do about the housing shortage?

John Prescott has just unveiled a raft of new planning guidance, claiming its plans will save 42 square miles of countryside, an area the size of Manchester. Mr Prescott has clearly listened to Lord Rogers. He has called for developers to build more small homes suitable for the growing singleton population, with the present density of 23 homes a hectare rising to 40.

Mr Prescott has also asked Gordon Brown, the chancellor, to impose VAT on all new house building. At the moment, no VAT is levied on building, but the full 17.5% rate is applied to the refurbishment of old properties. Lord Rogers called for VAT reform to encourage the conversion of existing buildings. The building lobby is fiercely opposed to any such move and the chancellor is thought to be sceptical.

Can brownfield development save the countryside?

Brownfield development – exploiting land already built on or used by industry – is frequently held to be the solution to bricking over the countryside. The Council for the Protection of Rural England has calculated that 8m people around England could be housed on urban derelict land if it were developed along the lines of traditional, relatively high-density, London streets and squares. London has room for 570,000 new homes without claiming a single green field.

Mr Prescott wants to build 60% of new homes on brownfield sites, encouraging the redevelopment of urban wasteland, which would also rejuvenate derelict and unattractive inner cities. But this is not terribly ambitious: the latest figures show that 56% of new homes are already being built on brownfield sites.

Brownfield building may be a worthy ideal, but it could be hard to attract people to live in such redevelopments. Demand for housing in the south-east has been rising largely because people move there to find work. Many brownfield sites, in areas such as East London, are not close to places of work. Developers need incentives to build on brownfield sites as making old industrial areas fit and safe for habitation is far more expensive than bricking up virgin fields.

Is the government doing enough?

Critics of all political hues tend to argue that the government is not doing enough to change Britain's wasteful house-building culture.

Liberal Democrat planning spokesman Mike Hancock argues that VAT on home improvements should be removed to encourage developers to bring the almost 1m empty houses in Britain back into use. The Liberal Democrats recommend grants to help meet the cost of clearing up brownfield sites and a tax on greenfield development to make it the more expensive option.

The Conservatives are trying to play the 'greener than thou' card. Shadow environment secretary Archie Norman responded to Mr Prescott's plans by saying: 'The real challenge is to convert our inner city accommodation so that it is suitable for elderly people living alone . . . not to migrate people out of our cities into the country, because that means the decline of the inner cities, as well as the permanent loss of the countryside.'

© Guardian Newspapers Limited, 2000

Town grouse and country grouse

How do you protect the countryside, build 1.1m new homes, revitalise cities and reverse the decline in the north? Answers to John Prescott

John Prescott is gearing up for the most important decision he might have to make as secretary of state for environment, transport and the regions. Rarely has an issue covered almost every aspect of his unwieldy empire: country towns bursting at the seams, roads permanently clogged up and builders threatening to carpet more greenfields with concrete and brick.

While tackling the country's crumbling railway infrastructure might have been foremost in his mind until Lord Macdonald began shouldering much of the transport brief, the deputy prime minister

By Peter Hetherington

knows development of the south-east – marginal middle-England, no less – could have far graver political consequences.

That's why No 10, and a key cabinet committee, has been mulling over housing projections and population forecasts for the ever-prospering region – England's wealthiest – as countryside campaigners and amenity groups flood local papers with protest letters, or take to the streets. The home counties, it seems,

are in revolt – partly because the issue has been so misrepresented.

Prescott's dilemma is how to balance rising demand for new homes, often from key workers such as nurses and teachers – and, increasingly, single people – with protecting the countryside and, crucially, meeting a target of putting up to 60% of new homes on recycled, or 'brownfield' land. The issue came to a head at a new style of planning inquiry in London last year. Two government inspectors 'tested' proposals from a planning consortium of local councils, known as Serplan, for a maximum of 914,000 homes in the 12 counties outside London up to 2016. Even this number, the planners conceded, would probably require a string of new townships and certainly a big expansion of Milton Keynes, in Buckinghamshire, to contain further greenfield building. Any more would require 'difficult environmental choices', warned Chris Williams, chairman of Serplan's strategy group.

Yet that's what the inspectors recommended to John Prescott last October: 1.1m homes, with new developments of 80,000-100,000 homes around Crawley in Sussex, Ashford in Kent, Stansted in Essex and Milton Keynes. Because they suggested building over a shorter timescale, the Council for the Protection of Rural England (CPRE) calculated this represented a 64% increase on Serplan's proposals, or 430,000 homes. It provoked a storm of protest, which has rarely subsided, and a string of lurid headlines – and cheap political gestures from the opposition – bearing little relation to reality.

Largely because of this uproar, the 1.1m figure became written in stone. It was portrayed as Prescott's plan, not as a recommendation which he could either accept, or reject. In fact, after intense discussions between Downing Street and his super-ministry, the deputy prime minister will steer a sensible, middle course, rejecting the old-fashioned, rigid 'predict and provide' approach to house building over long time frames in favour of a more flexible system looking no more than five years ahead – with regular, five-yearly reviews afterwards. He will opt for a big expansion of the Thames Gateway area, from Greenwich east to Dartford and Medway – where there is considerable 'brownfield' land – and earmark Ashford as a major growth point, conveniently sited for the Channel tunnel.

Nick Raynsford, his housing minister, has already signalled much tougher planning guidelines for local councils. Under these, developers will be subject to a series of rigorous, sequential tests. They will have to prove there is no brownfield land available in a particular area before being allowed to eye greenfield sites.

Crucially, they will also have to radically improve the design and standards of new houses – generally regarded by the minister as 'tacky little boxes' – and cram many more on to building sites. Raynsford says far too much land is wasted, further extending the urban sprawl.

But Prescott has another problem, often conveniently forgotten by the countryside lobby. While tens of thousands annually leave the sluggish north for work in the booming south-east, much of the housing demand is generated from within the region. Consequently, over the next 25 years, around 850,000 additional households are expected – and not all of them will be in a position to buy. This raises a further dilemma: the desperate shortage of lower cost, rented accommodation for people on average incomes, including young professionals. With house prices already five times average earnings in the region, even senior Tory councillors privately recognise that many more 'social' homes will be needed – perhaps 40% of planned provision – to cope with demand.

As he prepares for a final decision, the deputy prime minister is also facing criticism from another quarter – the old planning lobby, which strongly backs the case for 1.1m new homes. It accuses Prescott of bowing to pressure from the countryside campaigners. David Lock, vice chairman of the Town and Country Planning Association, accuses them of a 'campaign of deliberate misrepresentation and personal vilification [against Prescott's planning inspectors], which unleashed the bigotry of ignorant bullies . . . ' He fears that Prescott will be forced into a policy of 'town cramming' because of impossibly high brownfield targets.

At the other extreme, Prescott has to try to satisfy the architect Lord Rogers of Riverside, whose (government-appointed) urban task force last year called for tough measures – a tax on greenfield building and tax brakes for urban development – to curb the rural drift and help the repopulation of cities.

The normally mild-mannered architect, a friend of Mr Prescott, is becoming frustrated. This week he wrote that the government's reaction to his report had been 'disappointingly negative'. Unless England faced reality and placed more emphasis on reviving conurbations, he warned that the south-east would become even more congested, while northern cities would continue to suffer migration 'and the blight of decline'.

© Guardian Newspapers Limited, 2000

Urban footprints

The future of our countryside depends on our towns and cities treading more lightly on the environment

Benefits of city development

High-quality urban development:

- makes the best use of scarce land resources
- increases the cost effectiveness of public transport
- reduces the loss of countryside
- provides a positive alternative to building which damages landscapes and habitats
- maintains urban populations
- supports urban facilities and services
- reduces the need for car travel
- is more energy efficient
- provides opportunities to live without a car or be less dependent on it
- reduces length of journeys
- improves the local environment of the vast majority of the population
- tackles the problem of urban dereliction
- provides homes where people live
- revitalises vacant buildings
- returns unfit homes to active use
- supports existing business investment
- makes positive use of empty offices and vacant industrial land
- improves town centres
- supports existing infrastructure.

The choice before us

Every day hundreds of people move out of our cities to live in rural towns and villages. Rural land is consumed by new housing, roads, shopping centres and commercial development. Car use is spiralling upwards and journeys are getting longer. Meanwhile we are failing to get the best out of our cities. Thousands of acres of urban land lie derelict and tens of thousands of buildings remain vacant.

This is a picture of how we are exploiting our land – the most valuable resource in this small and overcrowded country. The distinction between town and country is becoming blurred and we are wasting scarce resources.

CPRE believes these trends cannot continue. The vital resource which our countryside represents for us all risks being lost for ever while our cities increasingly stand as monuments to neglect.

People's desire to live and work in the countryside is not surprising. People are more mobile than they have ever been and the attractions of rural life are obvious. But we cannot all move out to the country any more than we can give up on the generations of human investment in the fabric of our cities. To accept these trends as inevitable would be to condemn both urban and rural England to a poorer environment.

Development and change is of course necessary in rural areas but the scale of current building pressures is much too high. For example, we need to provide hundreds of thousands of new homes in England just to meet the requirements of the current population; but since nearly 80% of the population live in towns and cities this is where we should focus most of our efforts. The countryside cannot and need not carry the weight of continuing dispersal.

The challenge is to find ways of meeting society's needs and aspirations without continually building over our countryside. We should make better use of the infrastructure we already have. Land use and planning policies for town and country should be considered together and patterns of new development encouraged which make best use of the land and other resources in both. We should celebrate and enhance all that makes cities attractive and provide people with a positive alternative to leaving town – a high-quality urban environment in which to live.

Urban footprints

All new development – urban or rural – has an impact on land and resources. The impact of a new housing estate extends far beyond the site where it is built. It can be traced to the quarries supplying the building bricks, the reservoirs providing the water for people's taps

and the landfill sites absorbing the rubbish. Its new residents will make different types of journeys to work or to the shops. They may put more cars on the roads or add to the pressure to widen them.

The nature and size of the 'footprint' generated by these and other impacts depends crucially on where and how the development takes place. We need to find policies and incentives to ensure new building takes place where its 'footprint' treads most lightly on the environment. In many places this can bring environmental improvements.

Focusing on the way we use and develop our cities is a crucial part of the answer. They are the source of most of the pressure for new development. But encouraging more and better quality development to locate in urban areas will require a renewed commitment by all those involved – central and local government, developers, pension funds and other investors – as well as the support of an active public.

Town cramming and tower blocks?

The environmental 'footprint' of our cities can be reduced without a return to 1960s tower blocks or the loss of important open space.

Tower blocks offer few environmental advantages and can have a damaging effect on urban communities. Despite appearances, high-rise blocks frequently house people at a lower density than the housing they replaced. Higher-density development can be provided by converting existing houses or building new homes in low-rise mixed-facility developments. Family homes can still have gardens and the street environment can be improved.

Open spaces are vital to the urban environment. Parks, playing fields and fragments of woodland in our cities need not be sacrificed for new building. Even if they were all developed they could only provide a fraction of our building needs but at a huge environmental and social cost. The bulk of new development should come from making better use of existing built-up areas and run-down land. Open land and urban wildspace

make urban living more attractive and provide an alternative to the long trek to the countryside.

Vibrant cities

Our cities present a planning conundrum. On the one hand they have the potential to house, employ, transport and support large numbers of people efficiently. On the other they contain large areas of wasted land and empty buildings and unnecessarily consume natural resources.

The bulk of the houses, factories, offices, shopping centres, theatres, libraries, and other developments needed by England's 46 million people needs to be provided in towns and cities. However desirable the countryside is as a place to live it could never accommodate all the needs of modern society without losing its own value to society – its identity, its value for recreation and relaxation, and its ability to produce agricultural products in an environmentally responsible way. This has already been recognised in strong Green Belt and other planning policies which have helped keep England's urban areas relatively compact and protected much agricultural land from development. So although we have problems, we also have a foundation on which to build a fresh approach for the 21st century.

But despite their advantages we are not making good use of our cities. The urban environment is too often blighted by empty homes, vacant buildings and derelict land. There is not enough investment in reclamation and reuse of land or buildings and cities lack the transport

facilities they deserve. And planning and other land-use policies for urban areas are too often geared to outdated thinking about car parking standards and building density which obstruct regeneration efforts.

High-quality urban development can bring real advantages for our cities, the countryside, and the wider environment. Revitalising the city does not have to mean a return to tower blocks or the sacrifice of important open space. High-density, low-rise development can provide a high-quality environment. Given the opportunity, our cities can constantly renew themselves and provide more capacity for new development than is often appreciated. Research for the Joseph Rowntree Foundation, for example, showed that even quite modest changes to current practice could double the capacity for housing development of the areas studied. Planners need to embrace the possibilities brought by higher-density housing development and a reduced dependence on the car.

We should celebrate the positive things about urban life – the built environment and the social, economic and cultural opportunities it provides – and do more to protect what remains of the green space in our towns. We need a new approach: a new optimism about the value to society of our towns and cities and a new determination to invest in them for the benefit of us all – today and in the future.

What can be done?

There is a lot we can do for our cities. Here are a few suggestions, showing how everyone has a role to play in improving the quality of our urban areas and protecting the countryside:

The Government
- refine planning controls, policies and tax incentives so as to encourage builders and businesses to focus on urban areas
- allow local authorities to do more to tackle vacancy and dereliction
- provide more funds
- issue planning guidance on cities and sustainability
- set national and regional objectives for reducing the rate of loss of countryside to new building

- discourage those who hoard vacant land and buildings

Local councils
- plan positively for every part or urban England
- remove obstacles (e.g. restrictive parking standards, maximum density policies) to the better use of urban land
- support community-based solutions
- help bring development to where it is needed
- protect networks of open space
- improve local leisure provision
- safeguard town centres
- provide employment, shopping and other facilities in suburban areas which do not have them
- provide pedestrian priority and car-free areas

Developers, landowners and commerce
- underpin the benefits of past investment in town centres
- contribute to the management of urban spaces and provision of public facilities for both economic and environmental reasons
- respond to the opportunities provided by government regeneration initiatives
- refurbish and convert as alternatives to new-build
- release vacant land
- avoid car-based development

Public services
- improve urban public transport
- provide high-quality local health care and education
- tie future strategies more closely to land-use plans

People
- press local councils and your MP for new policies and funds to improve the urban environment
- prepare community strategies for your neighbourhood
- highlight areas of dereliction and decay and opportunities for enhancement and development
- demand a positive response
- celebrate the positive aspects of city life.

- The above is an extract from *Urban Footprints*, which is produced by the Council for the Protection of Rural England (CPRE). See page 41 for address details.

© Council for the Protection of Rural England (CPRE)

Room to live

Places for people

We are told our towns and cities are threatened by 'town-cramming'. Nothing could be further from the truth.

Vast tracts of urban England lie half-empty, sapped of vitality by the urban exodus of people and businesses to the countryside. Now the Government says it wants an Urban Renaissance. The challenge we face is how to revitalise our towns and cities with people, green spaces, safe streets and the best design so they become places where more of us choose to live.

Wasted spaces
Graffiti, crime, litter, and miles from work or the shops – the classic tower block image. But too often we mistake poverty, neglect and bad management for overcrowding. Far from being 'crammed', these high-rise estates were often built at lower densities than our prized Georgian streets and squares. We need to see higher densities as an opportunity, not a cost. All it takes is good planning, intelligent design and decent services.

The average density of new UK housing (9 houses per acre) is barely half that needed for a viable bus service (17 houses per acre).

Parklife
Urban living needs spaces where we can go to relax and hear ourselves think: the magnificent parks and squares of the past, allotments, new pocket parks on the doorstep and urban wild space. We need to make room for untidy spaces as well as neat ones. We have to value these precious green spaces more and give them stronger protection.

The costs of sprawl
Just like tower blocks, today's suburban estates also often create endless cul-de-sac mazes with no sense of place. They house too few people, not too many. Low-density housing wastes land, lacks life, supports few services, and forces people into their cars. We need to address how we can bring life to these soulless suburbs too.

Housing 4.4 million new households would require: 200 square miles of metropolitan Paris, or 300 square miles of Kensington and Chelsea in London, or 6,350 square miles of Milton Keynes.

Restored to life
Across the country and abroad, go-ahead planners, councillors and local communities are creating new and rejuvenated urban places of which their communities can be proud. The community-based regeneration of Hoxton in inner London shows what can be done to bring the city back to life.

Every little thing you need

Attracting people back into our towns and cities, with good design and green space, can help achieve vital, vibrant places. Neighbours, shops, schools, workshops, churches, offices, pubs, cafés, entertainment, open spaces – all on your doorstep, within easy walking distance or a short bus or bike ride away.

Our urban wasteland could house 3.2 million people at current densities of new building or 8 million (3.3 million households) as traditional London streets and squares.

Making room to live

Our towns and cities have been losing people and jobs for decades. 1,700 people a week are leaving our major cities for market towns and villages in the countryside. As the people go, so does urban life and prosperity. Shops close, jobs and services dwindle, commuter traffic increases and public transport struggles to survive.

The result is social exclusion and environmental decay. Yet urban England has space to spare, while in the countryside urban sprawl continues with 70 square miles of countryside built over each year.

To break this cycle of decline we need to harness new development and housing to improve our towns and cities. Yet many urban councils appear resistant to change, despite the potential benefits from extra resources and increased prosperity and civic pride.

Claims that 'the space isn't there' for more houses misunderstand the nature of urban capacity. It is a dynamic process, in which new redevelopment opportunities constantly appear to replace those already taken up.

At the root of much of the resistance to new housing in urban England has been a fear of 'town-cramming'. Yet density should never be confused with intensity. A dense town can be as spacious as any suburb. It is people alone who bring life to our towns and cities, and the density of houses, shops, work and leisure that makes up their vital parts.

Planners, politicians and developers need to seize the opportu-

The challenge we face is how to revitalise our towns and cities with people, green spaces, safe streets and the best design so they become places where more of us choose to live

nities for better environments which imaginative design can bring. We can unlock the potential of centres and suburbs to provide more variety, opportunity and convenience. We have to civilise the car and reclaim the urban parking prairies. We also need to renew our neglected urban fabric, and make new developments places to enjoy and be proud of. Above all we can use higher housing densities as a positive tool to secure vitality, safer streets, less pollution, better services and more prosperity.

More people living in urban areas will help:
- revitalise run-down places;
- support more jobs;
- improve safety;
- stimulate better services;
- maintain public transport;
- encourage a civil society;
- increase economic prosperity.

Councillors, planners and developers can act now to make more of urban space for living:

1. Use density as a positive tool
Include minimum density policies for all new development in your Unitary Development Plan or Local Plan

2. Banish the builders' boxes
Use urban design guidance to demand the best design from developers and make places that people can be proud of

3. Tackle traffic
Introduce lower speed limits and set targets in Local Transport Plans for traffic reduction to improve air quality and urban life

4. Curb parking
Limit the number of parking spaces required for new development and building conversions to free land for other uses

5. Save open space
Protect the networks of parks, gardens, green corridors, allotments and wild space which are the green lungs of urban life

6. Put pedestrians first
Make routes for walking and cycling more important than roads for getting around town

7. Mix living, work and leisure
Encourage and require mixed use in new development so shops and work can be just around the corner

8. Fill empty property
Produce an action plan to make better use of spaces over shops and offices and restore life to the centre of towns and cities

9. See the big picture
Use strategic urban design to lead change, for example by linking and managing the spaces between buildings

10. Know your potential
Carry out an urban capacity study to audit the potential for reuse, development and conversion

References
Bibby and Shepherd, Barton, quoted in Rudlin and the Urban and Economic Development Group (URBED):
Tomorrow: a peaceful path to urban reform, FOE/URBED/WISE, 1998
Office for National Statistics:
Regional Trends 33, The Stationery Office, 1998
Quid 98, Frémy Laffont, 1998

• CPRE is a national charity which helps people to protect their local countryside where there is threat, to enhance it where there is opportunity, and to keep it beautiful, productive and enjoyable for everyone.

CPRE works for a beautiful and living countryside on behalf of present and future generations, and for the more sustainable use of land and other resources in town and country. See page 41 for address details.

© *Council for the Protection of Rural England (CPRE)*

Housing people and protecting the environment

Planning and building sustainable communities

The current debate about how we might meet the housing needs of the estimated 4.4 million additional households is getting much media coverage. As the body which represents the independent social housing sector (housing associations, trusts and other independent not-for-profit landlords) the National Housing Federation is naturally interested in the debate.

We recognise that protecting the environment is an important aim, but so is providing a decent home for all in our communities.

Green spaces make a vital contribution to life in both urban and rural contexts, but the current debate is in danger of becoming too narrowly focused – of becoming a 'countryside versus development' debate.

Such a view is too simplistic and ignores the facts about land supply, household growth, employment and access to decent housing.

The National Housing Federation has produced this article to illustrate how it can be possible to meet the demand for new affordable housing in a sustainable way. Four areas of consideration are outlined:
- changes to the planning system
- the balance of incentives
- matching need and land
- a commitment to affordable housing.

Housing need

The projected increase in households serves to focus the minds of politicians and policy makers on the need for a strategy. Whilst there is discussion about the exact numbers of households that 2016 will see, the current debates appear to ignore that Britain currently has a substantial housing problem, which any increased growth will exacerbate.

This problem is faced not by those who can afford to buy, whether they be developments in the countryside or not, but rather those on low incomes. People who lack economic power and rely on affordable rented housing – the housing provided by Federation members.

We recognise that protecting the environment is an important aim, but so is providing a decent home for all in our communities

---

Regional needs

There are substantial variations in demand around the country. In some areas, especially in the south, new developments are needed, and there are clearly questions as to whether or not this can be achieved by only using existing land.

In other areas, there is a lack of demand for housing, for instance, due to migration out of cities for various reasons. Encouraging a return to the cities and regenerating urban areas is a real agenda.

Thus, the question of where shall the new households live is not a simple one. It is a complex balance between local need, available land and sites for redevelopment and regeneration, other factors including jobs, transport and amenities.

Current needs

- the Federation estimates that 95,000 affordable homes are needed each year between 2001 and 2016.
- there is an estimated backlog of need for 600,000 affordable homes – people who have no accommodation, live in temporary accommodation or housing that is unsuitable for a range of reasons.

- In the last seven years (1991-97/98) social landlords have provided 55,000 homes a year (on average). This results in a continual shortfall of homes and needs mount up.

These basic facts indicate the scale of the problem. It is estimated that 40% of the new households will be on low incomes. This creates a particular demand for affordable housing to rent.

Social landlords have to consider the needs of their tenants and of whole communities, in addition to having consideration for the environment. This means developing communities which are balanced, sustainable and which respond to local needs. In the main, we believe that this can be achieved without extensive damage to the countryside.

Responding to need

The Federation has four key considerations which it believes are necessary to tackle existing and projected levels of need in a sustainable and strategic way.

Planning system

Planning mechanisms must be changed and strengthened to ensure that local need is met in a way that could maximise the use of existing land. For instance, improving the link between regional guidance and local plans enables a more strategic approach not only to providing affordable housing but also land use. More flexibility and creativity on the use and recyling of available land will relieve pressure on greenfield sites whilst, at the same time, helping meet housing need.

Planning mechanisms are key to ensuring affordable housing is developed, and, at a regional level, should include specific reference to the requirements of affordable housing. At present there is no means of translating the national levels of need for affordable housing to regional and local level.

There must be sufficient affordable housing available, even if the needs are different. In rural areas, with pressure on house prices from commuters or people seeking to move to the country, local families cannot

afford to buy homes. In urban areas, affordable housing included in private developments helps to create more mixed communities and combat social exclusion.

Incentives

To use land effectively, a balance of measures are needed.

Positive incentives can ensure best use is made of existing land, derelict properties are developed and the quality of existing housing is improved. Reducing VAT on renovation is one clear instance of this, and is relevant to both rural and urban areas.

A greenfield tax sounds an effective way of limiting land use. However, it does not tackle the fact that brownfield sites incur clearance and other costs and are more expensive to develop. Likewise, a tax on all new housing in rural areas could result in a lack of affordable housing being built – affecting local people on low incomes.

Building at higher densities could realise up to 300,000 extra

---

Social housing to rent is not simply housing for the poor. For a percentage of the population, and for 40% of the projected new households, it is a necessity

---

dwellings over the next 20 years on brownfield sites, again relieving pressure on greenfield sites. This, however, requires a co-ordination of social and public services, transport and economic infrastructures otherwise people will not want to live or stay in them.

Matching need and land

Demand for housing is based on a number of factors, social and behavioural, aspirational, and particularly economic. Where migration from the cities takes place, the root causes need to be addressed. Local housing developments can rejuvenate city centres and make them attractive to communities, especially if they include employment.

In some pockets, particularly in the south, the demand cannot be met on brownfield sites or by urban regeneration alone. In these instances, use of greenfield sites has to be planned and strategic. Where necessary, new settlements, strategically planned to meet local need, with sufficient transport, employment and amenities may be a better use of greenfield sites than to continue extending existing towns.

Affordability

Social housing to rent is not simply housing for the poor. For a percentage of the population, and for 40% of the projected new households, it is a necessity. However, in the right locations, it is key to creating sustainable communities.

A commitment to developing affordable housing, through both planning and subsidy mechanisms, will not only tackle housing need, but can also help meet other social objectives. High rents, for instance, prohibit people being able to move from welfare to work.

Affordable housing can play a vital role in making the maximum use of land, meeting housing need and regenerating communities. Housing 4.4 million households need not mean vaste swathes of concrete – it can mean lively and vibrant communities. However, the commitment has to be there, supported by planning mechanisms and resources in place.

© *National Housing Federation*

Plans and planning

Information from the Wildlife Trust

In a small crowded country like ours, we have to resolve competition for space, so that many different needs – for housing, transport, services, open space and so on – are met. Planners have the difficult task of controlling our use of land, and although they regard nature conservation as important, they often decide that other interests should take priority.

In 1947, the Town and Country Planning Act introduced a requirement to obtain planning permission for 'developments'. Development was defined as the 'carrying out of building, engineering, mining or other operations over or under land' or 'the making of a material change of use to buildings or land'. Some developments, however, are outside planning control. Small alterations to dwellings may not require planning permission, and many agricultural and forestry developments are exempt. In addition, changes in the use of buildings, and work carried out by the statutory undertakers (e.g. gas and electricity companies) are not always controlled by planning legislation.

The planning system is designed so that applications can be dealt with in a consistent and objective way.

Planning policy guidance notes

From time to time, central government issues planning policy guidance notices (PPGs) to the local and regional authorities. These policy statements, available from HMSO bookshops, guide the decisions of planning departments. Particularly relevant to conservation are:
- PPG1 General policies and principles
- PPG2 Green belts
- PPG7 Countryside and the rural economy
- PPG9 Nature conservation
- PPG12 Development plans and regional planning guidance

PPG1 states that there must always be a general presumption in favour of a development, unless 'material considerations' indicate otherwise. This means that when wildlife is threatened, conservationists must show that their concerns are significant enough to override this general presumption. Government guidance does acknowledge that specially designated areas of nature conservation interest can be very important. International designations (Special Protection Areas, Special Areas of Conservation and RAMSAR sites – wetland areas named in the convention held at Ramsar in Iran, for example) are considered the highest tier of importance, followed by national designations (Sites of Special Scientific Interest, National Nature Reserves and National Parks). Effects of a development on wildlife sites of local importance are also a planning consideration.

PPG9 states that 'Nature conservation is a significant material consideration in determining many planning applications especially in or near SSSIs . . . '

Development plans

The Town and Country Planning Act 1990 sets out the framework of a plan-led system. As a rule, planning decisions should be taken in accordance with the statutory development plan. County Councils, Scottish Regional Councils and some National Parks prepare plans that cover large areas. Local plans show the detailed planning policies applied by the local authority. You can see plans that affect your area at your local and regional council, and in some libraries.

Development plans are very important, and the public's comments are sought before they are adopted. If conflicts cannot be resolved, a public inquiry is held, where a government inspector considers the objections made.

PPG12 put 'sustainable development' at the heart of forward planning. The Guidance states that the preparation of development plans can contribute to the objective of ensuring that development and growth are sustainable, and instructs local authorities to 'continue to develop (planning) policies consistent with the concept of sustainable development'.

Development control

Depending on the application, the decision to award planning permission can be taken by local elected representatives of the planning committee, the development control officer of the local authority or by government ministers. If planning permission is refused, developers can appeal against the decision to the Secretary of State. If planning permission is granted however, the people who think that it should have been refused do NOT have the right of appeal. Objections must be made before the decision is taken, and will be considered if relevant.

A list of the applications in your area – the planning register – can be inspected at the planning department. Your local wildlife trust comments on applications that affect nature conservation, and you may be able to get more information about local planning from them.

© The Wildlife Trust

Waiting for Lord Rogers's urban renaissance

The government's new urban policy will fail unless it can encourage more private skills and capital to help the poorer parts of Britain's cities

The government's long-awaited strategy for Britain's cities is finally to be published this autumn. In the past 40 years jobs and people have drifted away from many of the old industrial centres – Manchester and Liverpool have lost almost 40% of their populations. Large parts of some northern inner cities are rundown and semi-abandoned, despite the fact that billions of pounds of government money has been pumped into them since 1945.

This week the government announced that even more money will be spent. The regeneration budget for poor areas next year will be £1.2 billion ($1.8 billion) – a 20% increase on the previous year. Much of this cash will find its way into inner-city projects, aimed at everything from tackling crime to renovating housing.

But public money has been tried before. A more interesting question is whether the government's urban-policy white paper, the first for 20 years, will embrace the new ideas outlined by a government-appointed task force headed by Lord Rogers, one of Britain's most famous architects. This made more than 100 recommendations aimed at achieving 'an urban renaissance'. But its central thrust came down to three points: a demand for renewed emphasis on the look and feel of cities, alongside traditional priorities like health and welfare policy; a suggestion that more incentives should be given to encourage private capital into depressed areas; and a renewed (and controversial) emphasis on the virtues of 'high-density' living, rather than the British suburban dream.

The report was widely acclaimed – not least by the government. But since then, hopes of significant change have eroded. As ministers have dickered and argued, the white paper has been repeatedly delayed.

The reasons are not hard to find. The Treasury, fearful as always about loss of control and revenue, is unenthusiastic about the kinds of tax changes suggested by Lord Rogers and his colleagues. It does not like the idea of 'urban priority areas' – depressed areas in which taxes on business would be cut. It is unenthusiastic about tax incentives to build on previously developed land (brownfield sites). It is hostile to the proposal that there should be a £500m fund over ten years to renovate derelict buildings and other urban eyesores. It is also opposed to the recommendation that tax should

---

It makes little sense to pour billions of pounds into education and health without improving the environment

---

be equalised on new and refurbished buildings. At present new buildings are exempt, whereas the restoration of empty, old buildings is subject to VAT (sales tax) at the maximum rate of 17.5%.

The government has committed itself to the goal that 60% of new housing should be built on brownfield sites by 2008. But that is unlikely to happen without the sort of fiscal incentives proposed by Lord Rogers. This point has been forcefully made to ministers, both by the task force and by MPs. The all-party parliamentary committee on the environment has said that it is 'disgraceful' that the Treasury had 'kicked the task force's report into the long grass'. The committee's report endorsed the task force's conclusion that urban regeneration would not happen without sharper incentives.

Lord Rogers himself is surprisingly philosophical. But he does argue that it makes little sense to pour billions of pounds into

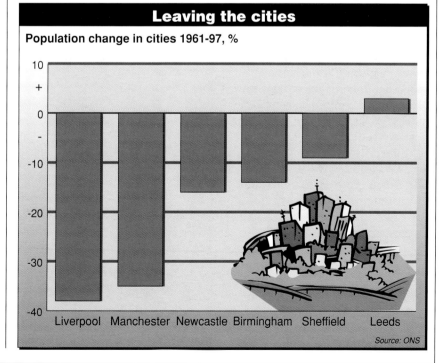

Leaving the cities

Population change in cities 1961-97, %

Liverpool   Manchester   Newcastle   Birmingham   Sheffield   Leeds

Source: ONS

education and health without improving the environment in which those services are delivered. Without a better quality of life in poor inner-city areas, professional people who deliver services will depart, leaving only the poorest behind. 'The physical and the social must go together,' he insists.

The task force may have lost its battle over tax incentives, but its report has been influential in other areas. Its argument for cities built to a high density has been reflected in the government's latest planning guidance, which says that preference should be given to compact developments on brownfield sites. Most recent housing has been built to very low densities, exacerbating urban sprawl. England has the lowest urban housing density in the European Union, at 23 households per hectare. In parts of east Manchester, for example, densities have fallen to eight per hectare. In some continental cities, such as Barcelona (a city whose virtues appears to obsess urban planners in Britain), the ratio of housing is ten to 50 times higher.

No English city even approaches these figures although England is among the most densely populated countries in the world. The British phobia about high-density housing is understandable given the disastrous record of many of the tower blocks put up in the post-war era, which have become a byword for ugliness, squalor and crime. But high-density need not be high-rise – it could mean fashionable loft apartments in converted warehouses, or new terraced housing around communal gardens. (As Lord Rogers points out: 'I have never heard anyone complaining of living in a Georgian terrace.') Similarly, low-density housing is by no means a guarantee of desirability or success. Some of the most notorious housing estates in Britain, like Halton Moor in Leeds, are largely made up of suburban-style houses, not tower blocks.

Lord Rogers's focus on the importance of clean, safe streets may also prove influential. The task force estimates that of the £200 billion of government money spent each year in English towns and cities – mostly on health, education and welfare

payments – less than 4% is spent on buildings and transport. Skimping on maintenance and security helps set in train a cycle of neglect. Mean, badly lit, crime-ridden streets covered in graffiti, litter and dog mess are the common experience of many poor residents. If the public sector were to spend more time and money tackling these problems in depressed urban areas, private businesses might be encouraged to invest more.

At the moment, people who live in poor urban estates are pessimistic about the future. A survey of council estates by the Joseph Rowntree Foundation in 1998 found that three times as many thought that their neighbourhood had got worse rather than better. A major concern is crime. The task force's report noted that 10% of residents in inner-city areas are burgled at least once a year,

twice as much as elsewhere. A quarter of ethnic-minority residents in low-income areas complained of racially motivated attacks on their families.

Some depressed inner-city areas have been turned round – but sometimes only after being razed. Hulme, in Manchester, a beneficiary of public funding, has been transformed: the existing buildings were demolished and then replaced by new mixed-income housing. Newcastle is about to demolish 6,600 homes in its poverty-stricken West End, to make way for new development costing more than £400m. More than half the cost will come from public funding.

Publicly-funded regeneration on this scale is not only costly, it also needs to be accompanied by private-sector development if it is to succeed. New urban regeneration companies have been formed in east Manchester, Liverpool and Sheffield to try to draw in new businesses. But they will have a much stronger chance of success if central government gives them the planning powers and tax incentives they are asking for. Depressed inner cities will be convincingly revived only when the private sector is willing and able to make it happen.

© The Economist Newspaper Limited, London, 5th August 2000. All Rights Reserved

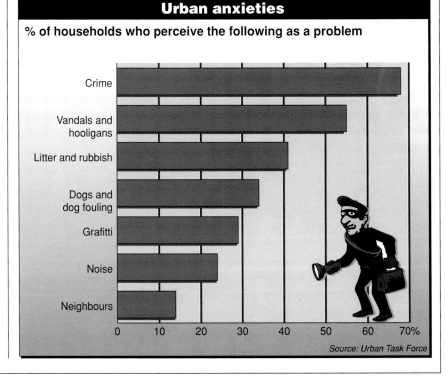

Urban anxieties

% of households who perceive the following as a problem

- Crime
- Vandals and hooligans
- Litter and rubbish
- Dogs and dog fouling
- Grafitti
- Noise
- Neighbours

0   10   20   30   40   50   60   70%

Source: Urban Task Force

Building and urban development

An interview with Lord Rogers

The architect Richard Rogers is so much at the heart of the new establishment in England that he is flanked by two official minders from the press office – a sign, if ever there was one, of status within government. He has a whole morning of interviews lined up to launch his Urban Task Force's recipe for the revitalisation of our cities.

Lord Rogers occupies a Georgian house in Chelsea, where all the riches of a great city are on his doorstep. We must make our cities work better. We must protect our countryside. Both these objectives would be achieved if the enjoyment that he finds in urban life could be shared with the public as a whole.

Strangely, his views coincide with those of John Simpson and others, whose stylistic preferences for Classicism are the polar opposite of his own. The trouble is, there is still a big selling job to be done on the public. How are they to be winkled out of their suburbs, or disabused of their dreams of a country existence? It will take a persuasive advocate indeed.

According to Rogers, the British have a great tradition of making cities. Then came the Industrial Revolution, and urban life 'became hell'. It was then that we developed our understandable obsession with the countryside. Utopians such as Ebenezer Howard initiated the Garden City and Garden Suburb movements. They resulted, ultimately, in Milton Keynes.

These days, most of the polluting industries have disappeared. Information technology, while freeing the individual from his reliance on a fixed place of work, seems, paradoxically, to encourage more interest in city living. Children leave home earlier. We live to the age of 100. We spend a far shorter proportion of our lives in rearing the young than we would

have done when families of 10 children were common. Demographically, the conditions for an urban renaissance are ripe.

By contrast, the city fabric is, in many places, rotten. Brownfield sites, such as these, must be developed. We must create cities in which it is possible to walk to the shops and bicycle to work. The areas where people live must be protected from traffic. Everyone should have access to an open space within 500m of their home. 'The pavement outside the house is where you really meet people. How do we make streets livable?' We do so, he continues, by controlling the number of cars.

Cities are increasingly vying with each other for a position on the world stage. London is in competition with Paris, Frankfurt, Tokyo, New York. As it happens, it is succeeding almost too well – one of the problems that the Urban Task Force does not seem to consider is the problems posed by the boom in the capital's property prices. By contrast, the cities of the North-East are stagnating. It is not just that British people do not

want to live in cities; they do not want to live in the cities where nothing is happening. They want to retire to Devon.

Lord Rogers' original brief was to assess how many of the new homes we are said to require could be built on brownfield sites. His answer is about 50% of them. Hence the campaign for cities. The best cities are those which have lots of people living closely together. In Barcelona, the figure is 400 per hectare. In the suburbs of London, it is as low as 25 per hectare. There are a number of subtexts to Rogers' message. One is that people in the suburbs had better budge up a bit. Another is that something really serious must be done about cars. So far, the Deputy Prime Minister has shown himself to be considerably more radical than the Prime Minister.

• The above is an extract from the online version of the magazine *Country Life*, which is produced by IPC Media Ltd. The online magazine can be found at www.countrylife.co.uk

© IPC Media Ltd

Halt greenfield housing

Information from Friends of the Earth

Government forecasts say 4.4 million new households may form in England by 2016. This is because young people are leaving home earlier, more people are getting divorced and people are living longer. The question of how and where these people will be housed is one of the most important environmental and social issues of the decade.

Since the war, Government policies have led more and more people to leave existing cities to live in suburbs and rural areas. This has caused huge swathes of the country to disappear under brick and concrete, and has undermined inner-city economies. It has also fuelled a massive increase in the use of cars, as people living in the countryside need to travel further, but have less access to public transport.

Now people are questioning this trend. More and more people, including architects, planners and environmentalists, believe we should encourage house-building on re-cycled land and discourage endless urban sprawl. This would not only protect the countryside but also help regenerate the inner cities and reduce car dependency.

John Prescott, the Secretary of State for the Environment, Transport and the Regions, has said he wants to take a more flexible approach to planning for new housing. However house-builders say recycled land is difficult to develop and are pushing forward with plans to build on greenfield sites. Friends of the Earth believes that three-quarters of the new homes needed should be provided within existing towns and cities.

A nation of individuals

The Government unleashed a political storm when it published a new set of household projections in 1995 suggesting that 4.4 million new households will form in England between 1991 and 2016. This is because young people are leaving home earlier and married couples are getting divorced more frequently. Additionally, the population of England is growing, partly because people are living longer, and partly because of migration into the country, including from other parts of the UK.

A household is defined as one or more people who live together. Going by recent trends, our traditional nuclear family is breaking up, and four-fifths of the new households are predicted to be single people. All these new households will create enormous pressure on the supply of new housing.

House-building versus the countryside

In the nineteenth century, industrialisation and population growth led to a massive expansion of cities like London, Birmingham, Manchester and Leeds. This un-planned growth led to appalling urban squalor and fuelled the 'garden cities movement' in support of lower housing densities and new settle-ments. As a result, much new housing was built on the edge of existing towns – as suburbs – and in villages or planned New Towns such as Milton Keynes. Between the wars, although their population hardly increased, major cities spread out massively as low-density suburbs were built around them. After the war, concern over Britain's expanding cities led to the designation of Green Belts around many of them. None-theless, since 1945 an area greater than the combined total of Greater London, Berkshire, Hertfordshire and Oxfordshire has been urbanised.

House-building on greenfield sites has become increasingly contro-versial as people recognise the need to protect the countryside and develop sustainably. Opposition to new house-building is particularly intense among rural communities, who feel the character of where they live is changing forever, and in suburban communities who fear that building on the Green Belt will cut them off from the countryside. The problem is made worse because most housing on greenfield sites is executive-type homes built at very low densities. It covers a lot of land, but houses relatively few people.

Over the next few years, as plans for house-building escalate, this opposition looks set to mushroom. John Gummer, then Conservative Environment Secretary, recognised this when he published a Green paper, *Household growth: where shall we live?* in November 1996. This suggested that more new homes should be provided on recycled land within existing towns and cities (i.e. land which has previously had some other use). Mr Gummer proposed to achieve this by raising the target for recycled land use to 60 per cent (from the existing 50 per cent), and bringing in new planning policies to favour urban locations for housing developments (like the so-called 'sequential' test).

The election of a Labour Government has only raised concern in rural and suburban communities further. Labour politicians were sceptical about providing more homes in cities before the election. The early track record of the new Government is not encouraging. John Prescott, the Secretary of State for the Environment, Transport and the Regions, ordered West Sussex County Council to increase its housing target by 12,800. He allowed Newcastle upon Tyne to designate land for 2,500 homes in the Green Belt, and more controversially, he refused to intervene in the release of Green Belt land to the west of Stevenage for 10,000 new homes.

The Stevenage decision made front-page news. It looks set to fan the flames of revolt over greenfield housing over large parts of England. Other controversial plans for housing have also generated intense local opposition, such as a proposed new town at Micheldever in Hampshire, and a scheme for housing on the recently designated battlefield of Tewkesbury in Gloucestershire.

These controversies are just the tip of the iceberg. The new household projections have yet to be in-corporated fully into local authority plans. When this happens local authorities will find themselves with massive and unachievable housing targets. Far larger areas of land will be sacrificed to house-building unless fundamental changes to planning policies are made.

Predict and provide

Planning for new housing is deeply flawed. Housing targets are imposed on local authorities through the so-called 'cascade' system, starting with the household projections, and cascading down through the regional, county and then district plans. Each level in the system is given an 'allocation' of houses to build. The process is heavily 'top-down', and takes little account of local circum-stances. There is no assessment of how many homes an area can take, or the environmental impact of the new housing.

The figures are supposed to be re-examined at the local level, to take account of uncertainties in the projections. However, in practice the Government has consistently inter-vened to impose figures on county councils.

The whole process has become a self-fulfilling prophecy, as the household projections are simply based on past trends. There is, for example, considerable evidence of a 'circularity effect', whereby the provision of new homes draws people into an area, leading to higher household projections and hence higher housing targets into the future.

Furthermore, there are major uncertainties in the household projections which are given little acknowledgement. As an example, household size is predicted to fall to 2.17 by 2016. This is a difficult prediction to make to such a degree of accuracy, as there has been a falling off recently in the decline of family size. If the figure varied by 0.1 (to 2.27), approximately one million fewer households would form. Clearly a more flexible approach is required.

Instead of the whole system being dominated by unrealistic housing targets, we need to determine policy from sensible objectives – protection of the countryside, regenerating our towns and cities and reducing traffic and congestion.

We also need more recognition of the different problems the regions face and the strategies they undertake

---

Most people live in towns and cities. It is undeniable that some want to move out in search of a better life

---

to solve them. The South-East faces the brunt of house-building, yet already has the greatest development pressures and traffic congestion. The South-West faces considerable pressures from in-migration, yet has relatively few brownfield sites for housing developments. In the North, urban decline is a major issue, as well as the poor quality of much of the existing housing stock.

Environmental disaster?

There is now widespread concern about the environmental implica-tions of greenfield house-building. Government figures suggest that over 169,000 hectares of countryside will fall between 1991 and 2016 – greater than the entire area of Surrey. Up to two million houses could be built on greenfields – equivalent to about four new cities the size of Birmingham.

One of the most worrying aspect of urban sprawl is all the new traffic which comes with it. People who live in suburbs or small settlements drive more. This not only increases congestion and pollution. It leaves people increasingly dependent on their cars to get to out-of-town shops and other developments. The poor especially suffer as local services decline.

New housing has a multitude of other environmental impacts. Energy use in houses accounts for 30 per cent of our total energy consumption, and we waste vast quantities of it. Our homes consume over ten times the energy of the state-of-the-art houses being built elsewhere in Europe. The spaced-out houses of suburban sprawl are far less efficient than traditional terrace design, yet are favoured by the building industry.

Households use up a third of the water supply in England. Over half the new housing (2.3 million homes) is planned for the worst drought-hit regions, the South-East and East. The Environment Agency is already warning of serious water supply problems.

New housing in the countryside also means new shopping centres, schools, roads, and all the other developments which follow. This is wasteful. Far better to use the existing facilities in towns and cities. We need a new agenda for urban renaissance.

An urban renaissance?

Most people live in towns and cities. It is undeniable that some want to move out in search of a better life. But the very act of building on greenfield sites destroys the landscapes people wish to move to. The only way to protect the countryside is to provide more homes in urban areas, and make towns and cities better places to live in. We must provide quality housing, as well as improve education, and tackle crime, traffic and noise.

In response to the prolonged debate in the media over greenfield house-building, the Labour Government has begun to promote urban renewal. In February 1998, Mr Prescott published *Planning for the Communities of the Future*, the first formal statement on housing and land-use policy. This set out proposals to 'help us achieve our twin aims of an urban renaissance and of ensuring a green and pleasant land we can hand on to future generations'.

John Prescott claimed he wanted to: 'replace the top-down "predict and provide" mentality of the past, with a system which is more responsive, more accountable, and better able to revitalise our towns and cities and protect a living countryside which we can all enjoy'. The most significant step was that the new policies should allow 'local planning authorities to be able to raise the national proportion of new homes to be built on previously developed land to 60 per cent over the next ten years'.

As a statement of intent, *Planning for the Communities of the Future* is welcome. But the details of the new planning regime it proposes have yet to be worked out. It gives no guarantee that huge swathes of countryside will not be built on, and does little to make recycled land in urban areas more attractive to house-builders.

There are many more opportunities for providing new homes in urban areas than appear at first sight. These include converting large houses and empty offices into flats, getting more people into the hundreds of thousands of houses sitting empty, and building new homes on recycled land. The table below suggests some options, based on the latest research findings.

Affordable housing

About 40 per cent of the people in the predicted new households will not be able to afford market housing. These households will require some form of subsidy or mechanism to gain access to housing. Yet at present, Government grants allow far fewer affordable homes than are needed. The poor suffer sub-standard or cramped accommodation as a result.

Unless the Government deals with this pressing issue, we risk allocating greenfield sites which are simply 'cherrypicked' for market housing – while ignoring the needs of poorer households. The Government must make much clearer connections between the allocation of land for housing, and the availability of funding for social housing.

Rural communities in particular depend on affordable rented housing. If this is restricted, then many who work in agriculture and local businesses will be forced to move to the cities, leaving predominantly wealthy people who commute to work and make little use of the local economy. We need affordable housing to keep the countryside alive.

Conclusions

There is clearly a need to provide substantial numbers of new dwellings. The real issue is where these homes will be located. We face a stark choice. Further greenfield developments would mean more suburbanisation, loss of countryside, congestion and car dependency. Or we could choose urban renaissance, protecting the countryside, and better public transport instead.

Policies set by central Government should use economic instruments and the planning system to encourage more medium-density housing in existing cities and discourage greenfield house-building. There is a clear need for more affordable housing through adequate funding and better planning mechanisms. In addition, Friends of the Earth is calling for the following specific policies:

Planning policies for regeneration:

- A challenging target for 75 per cent of new housing to be provided within existing urban areas, with regional targets as appropriate;
- A flexible approach to housing numbers, so they are decided at a more local level, and are not

Providing new homes	
Urban capacity option	**Additional homes[1]**
a. Reduced vacancy rates	325,000
b. Conversions to flats	380,000
c. Commercial space & LOTs	80,000
d. Building on recycled land	2,217,000
e. Planned regeneration	246,000
f. Under-used car parks	160,000
Total[2]	**3,408,000**

[1] Data from *Tomorrow: A Peaceful Path to Urban Reform*. Similar findings based on comparable assumptions were published in *Tomorrow's World* by Friends of the Earth in 1997.

[2] Approximately 850,000 homes have already been built from 1991-1998.

a. The Empty Homes Agency says that almost 800,000 homes stand empty in England.
b. Lower parking requirements would allow more flat conversions. (Llewellyn Davies, 1994.)
c. Living over the Shop (LOTS) schemes have considerable potential to provide more homes.
d. Based on surveys of vacant and derelict land.
e. Intensification of urban areas and redevelopment of council estates.
f. Based on new research by TELLUS 42.

Source: Friends of the Earth

imposed by central Government;

- A presumption against greenfield developments, and favouring new housing on recycled land in urban areas through a sequential and phased approach to the release of land;
- Planning policies to encourage more medium-density housing in existing cities, especially around public transport nodes;
- Reduced car parking provision for new housing, with maximum rather than minimum standards.

Fiscal policies for regeneration:

- A greenfield tax or other similar levy;
- Value added tax to be harmonised between new-build (which is currently free of VAT) and restoration or refurbishment;
- Grants for the assembly and conversion of urban land, plus new programmes for home improvement and conversions;
- Taxation of car parking spaces

(especially private non-residential);

- An end to the Council Tax rebate on empty homes.

What you can do

- Using the information here, write to your MP outlining your opposition to further greenfield housing development, and reinforce the need to provide more housing in towns and cities.
- Get involved in the local fight against greenfield house-building. Order a copy of our invaluable 40-page campaign guide *Stopping the Sprawl* through FOE Publications Despatch, 56-58 Alma St, LUTON, LU1 2PH (with cheque or credit card details). Or call 020 7490 1555. Price £7.00 (incl. P&P). Quote code L417.
- Urge your county council to resist impossible Government targets for house-building, and urge your local council to put a stop to out-of-town developments.
- Send us brief details of any local

greenfield developments to add to our database. Let us know the name of the site, the precise location, the number of houses to be built, the name of the local authority, and local contact details.

- Get your local campaign group to join 'URGENT' (the Urban Regeneration and Greenfield Network), the new network to promote sustainable housing policies. Visit the URGENT website at www.urgent.org.uk
- Join FOE local groups fighting to halt urban sprawl and aid urban renewal in your area. Call 0990 22 44 88.
- Order *Tomorrow: A Peaceful Path to Urban Reform* from FOE Publications Despatch (as above). Price £8.00 (incl. P&P). Quote code L434. This is a comprehensive guide to the household growth debate, the environmental implications of greenfield developments, and how we can achieve the sustainable alternative – an urban renaissance.

© Friends of the Earth

What's behind the 4.4 million extra households?

Information from the Green Party of England and Wales

What?

Back in 1995 a report for the Department of the Environment claimed that in the 25 years between 1991 and 2016 there would be a 4.4 million increase (23%) in the number of households in England, from 19.2 million to 23.6 million. This however is no different from similar preceding periods and 90% of this growth has already been assumed and provided for in existing structure plans, at least up until 2006. However, the ensuing spotlight on more household growth has focused large-scale attention on its implications for land use, the environment and social justice.

The figures have also been challenged by various housing and research organisations for not including the backlog of unmet need

(as well as not enough homes being built between 1991 and 1998), nor the replacement of those buildings being demolished. This has been calculated to add a further million. Figures relating to the numbers of houses which subsequently need to be built annually also vary. Using the DoE figures, roughly 200,000 new homes need to be built annually until 2016. However a more recent government report states this should be 175,000 per year. This compares with around 150,000 dwellings built over each of the past three years, slightly more than in the first 3 years of the 1990s but less than in the boom years of the 60s when building peaked at 300,000 homes a year. It also needs to be borne in mind that 1.3 million homes have been built since 1991.

Why?

The government's research claims that this increase is partly due to a projected 3.6 million increase in population. These figures are based on current trends and assumptions about how this new population will divide into different households, as well as assumptions about internal and external migration and immigration. 21% of the extra number of households are expected from the increase in the numbers of elderly people, as they live longer, with another 33% from behavioural changes. This reflects the trend since the beginning of the century for households to continue getting smaller. 80% are expected to be one-person households, through people leaving home earlier, people not marrying or having children until later in life, and more people divorcing. Of these it is projected that the greatest increase will be in male one person households. However, previous social and economic trends, on which these assumptions are based, are always open to change.

Where?

It is also projected that land in England given over to urban use will rise from 10.6% in 1991 to 11.9% in 2016, although this does not reflect the proportion of land that is thus blighted by adjoining urban development. There is still an underlying trend for people to want to leave the cities and find work and homes in more rural areas so those who have a choice in moving will add to the pressure on greenbelt and greenfield sites around existing rural settlements. The government has stated the current 50% rate of building on brownfield sites, whether urban or non urban, should increase to at least 60%. The government-appointed UK Roundtable on Sustainable Development as well as the Council for the Protection of Rural England (CPRE) and FoE state it should be possible to aim for a 75% rate. If the total number of new homes needed is over 5 million then even with 60% being on brownfield sites, it would mean 2 million new homes on greenfield sites.

The government's recently appointed Urban Task Force, led by the architect Richard Rogers, is looking specifically into how best to use previously developed land. It will make its final report in summer 1999. The issue of who is going to pay for the decontamination of contaminated land in order for some of these sites to be useable is not yet resolved, but local authorities will be required by law from summer to be more proactive here.

If the total number of new homes needed is over 5 million then even with 60% being on brownfield sites, it would mean 2 million new homes on greenfield sites

---

Regions are predicted to suffer differentially, through assumptions about migration trends. The highest % increase is projected to be in the South West and East (29% each), South East (27%) and E Midlands (26%). The projected growth is more of a serious issue in the already overcrowded South and East with 'overheating' and huge pressure on green belt land. Whereas in the North, where overall growth (in the more rural parts) is also predicted (between 12.5% and 19%), there are worse housing conditions and in many urban areas a new and severe problem with low demand, particularly for 'social' housing, resulting in an increase in empty and difficult-to-let properties, even new ones, something relatively unknown in the South and East.

Housing for all?

Just over 20% of the current housing stock is in the public sector (i.e. housing primarily for those on low incomes or in need of support), either through local authorities or registered social landlords. This compares with 23% in 1991 and 31% in 1979. To make up for unmet need in this sector at least 40% of the DoE's figures need to be affordable, social housing. This means about 100,000 annually, a figure which housing organisations say has been needed, but not provided, for many years. The government's own environment select committee state between 60,000 and 100,000 are needed annually. Yet, only around 30,000 are being produced per year with 37,000 projected to be built for 1999/2000. However, these figures do not account for the shortfall in building for unmet needs over the past decade or so. Recent research by Shelter concludes that, in fact, over 150,000 affordable homes need to be built, or made available, annually up to 2006 to meet three-quarters of rising and unmet demand, taking into account the limited amount of building prior to 1997. This would necessitate five times the current building rate for social housing. Despite the acknowledged need, social housing targets or housing types are not adopted in

the Regional Planning Guidance, and rarely in structure and local plans, so there is no guarantee that the housing built will reflect local need in terms of affordability or dwelling size.

This should be seen in the context of a reduction in government investment in housing over the past 6 years, with this year's expenditure only half that of 1992 despite the long-awaited release of capital receipts from the past sale of 2 million of the most popular council homes. The rate of UK investment in housing is already, over the last decade, the lowest of EU economies.

Additionally, there are now 750,000 empty homes – 3.7% of all stock at 1 April 1997 – hardly any change since 1991. While many are vacant due to the normal 'transaction' period between moving, 250,000 of these could be rented out straight away with a little encouragement. 7.5% of all stock (1.5 million dwellings) is unfit for human habitation, the same as in 1991. A further 3.8 million dwellings need urgent repair. 14.2% of households live in poor housing (i.e. either unfit, in substantial disrepair or requires essential modernisation) with private tenants more likely to (31%). The previous government's policies of cutting back financial support have forced housing associations to charge rents near to market levels, which together with the current benefit system have contributed to the process of social exclusion through the concentration of people dependent on benefits and/or caught in the benefit trap and the decline in popularity of social housing.

Rural versus urban

A quarter of the household increase is projected to be in the rural areas, with an even greater proportion than the average being single-person households, almost all of which will be aged over 30 years old. Homelessness is underestimated in rural areas where it is rising faster than in urban areas. However research in 1996 revealed that most local authorities had not undertaken a housing needs survey that distinguished rural needs. There is already a smaller proportion of social housing available here than the

English average, and with high rents being charged by much of the new social housing, many potential tenants in low paid employment have been forced to move to more urban areas.

Building and craft quality

There is also concern about the quality of current building standards along with concern about the availability and quality of craft training within the building industry. In 1997 the Building Employers' Confederation and Further Education Funding Council inspectorate were saying that there would be a shortage in the next century of trained craftspeople in the building trade. There needs to be more investment in quality training and apprenticeships. Over 500,000 construction jobs have been lost since 1990 and training levels have been low. There is a great need for more investment into better quality, longer-lasting housing as well as quality repair and renovation of older stock. Nearly half of all stock is over 50 years old and at current rates of replacement will have to last 5,600 years. The legal building regulations still have low-level standards of energy and thermal efficiency, sound insulation and other ecological and human sensitive design considerations.

FLASHPOINT examples
There are many areas around the country – these are just a few:
- large areas around Stroud in Gloucestershire under threat
- Victoria Jubilee allotments (18-acre site) in Handsworth, Birmingham, under threat
- Stevenage – plans approved for a new settlement of over 10,000 homes on green belt land
- 2,000 houses to be built on green belt land outside Newcastle, even

---

Homelessness is underestimated in rural areas where it is rising faster than in urban areas

---

though 75% of new homes to be built on brown land in the urban area and in area of low demand for public sector housing
- Cambridgeshire – proposed new town site
- East Kent – in the already overpopulated South East over 100,000 new homes to be built, including 20,000 around the new Bluewater shopping development in the former Blue Circle quarries at Dartford

Some organisational responses
DETR's Select Committee 10th Report (Housing) 1998
- environmental protection and sustainable development should be at the centre of housing policies. Need to consider local water supply
- extend existing urban areas rather than new settlements. Strict greenfield restrictions and a green field levy which would not prevent the building of social housing in rural areas
- at least 60% brownfield site development, with regional variations possible e.g. nearly 100% in London. Public investment to make brownfield sites suitable. Heavier taxation on urban car parking space
- better use made of empty homes and existing buildings. No VAT on conversions
- clarify the different roles and powers of the Regional Development Agencies, regional chambers, regional planning conferences, and the Government Offices of the Regions in relation to housing and planning
- clear sustainability criteria to measure the effects of potential developments; revision of PPG3 to include more stringent environment and land use measures. (PPG3 consultation draft now out)

Civic Trust
- Issue is about quality not density
- important to ensure the emphasis on social housing needs is kept up, within framework of support for mixed communities, jobs and transport considerations

Local Government Association (LGA)

- better co-ordination of work of planning and housing departments
- more government resources to meet the shortfall in existing affordable housing
- change the current approach to local and regional household projections and housing need with a more decentralised and 'bottom-up' approach, through local plans in partnership with local communities. Stipulate housing type as well as whether private or within the social housing sector
- 60% target in sustainable brownfield locations. Otherwise on edge of existing towns and villages
- LAs should adopt and pursue empty housing strategies and imaginative ways of developing higher density and quality housing in urban areas
- review the charging of VAT on house conversions and look into a greenfield tax.

Town and Country Planning Association (TCPA)

- supports the idea of a new generation of new towns in certain regions, except the South East, and clustered developments along rail corridors
- need to protect existing urban greenfield sites
- look into alternatives to houses for many of the single-person households
- more emphasis should be on policy development rather than responding to projections from past behaviour patterns e.g. regional migration
- doubtful about being able to do much more with brownfield sites, many of which won't have access to transport, employment and other facilities that other selected greenfield sites already have.

House Builders' Federation (HBF)

- projections are not substantially greater than current building rates – what is all the fuss?
- ease planning restrictions on green field sites
- land prices need to come down. New towns OK

- tax sale of agricultural land with planning permission for development. Monies raised to release more brownfield sites.

Shelter

- not enough planning for social housing – must not rely just on market forces for those that can buy or pay high rent
- much more resources needed from central government. Joined-up solutions needed most here, especially with planning and housing
- needs to be a standardised method of assessing housing need at the local level by housing type and tenure. Local authorities to develop clear action plan to meet the affordable housing targets.

Friends of the Earth (FoE)

- opposed to top-down housing targets – more autonomy to local authority in deciding housing need
- need for greater density in existing urban areas, more emphasis on urban regeneration with traffic reduction
- sequential approach
- 75% target for brownfield sites
- financial help to bring together and make safe urban land. Greenfield tax or similar
- VAT harmonisation between new build and conversions/refurbishment

---

- end to council tax rebate on empty homes.

Council for the Protection of Rural England (CPRE)

- serious environment and social problems from current approach to planning for housing need
- therefore local planning and housing departments to work more closely together to produce better phasing of development which better reflects housing need and range of house types.

National Housing Federation (NHF)

- housing and planning departments should work through one directorate, with planning mechanisms strengthened to ensure the meeting of affordable housing targets
- social and affordable housing given priority in the strategies of the new regional agencies/chambers
- integration of housing development with social, economic and physical infrastructure.

Some extracts from current Green Party policy:

- Housing policy should be fully integrated with other polices to build more sustainable, self-reliant communities(HO305). Everyone should be provided with housing appropriate to their needs (HO201)

- Emphasis on local provision for local needs, with more decentralised forms of housing management. Housing Associations encouraged to become smaller (HO104). Housing co-ops should be encouraged as effective providers of low-cost housing, with the setting up of a new Co-operative Housing Agency (HO106, HO409)
- local authorities to have more autonomy in social housing provision through the development of more self-reliant economies and the levying of a greater proportion of taxation locally (HO403)
- current housing subsidy and benefits system unfair – to be integrated with Citizens Income (HO402)

- as far as possible no new development on any more agricultural land or land outside the confines of an urban or village area (B400). A Land Value Tax (as a substitute for other taxes) on the annual value of the land is proposed, helping to reduce speculation – investment in buildings should benefit the whole community not just the individuals who own them (HO401; LD203; LD206), with a locally determined and democratically accountable land use planning system (LD302) (LD400)
- planning process to be made more democratic and accessible – for larger schemes and proposed developments on greenfield sites, independent comprehensive environmental

impact assessments needed (HO503)
- priority given to the maintenance and improvement of existing buildings before new house building considered (H0411); better use made of existing buildings; new buildings to be built to improved standards for accessibility, space and facilities, ergonomics, sound and thermal insulation and energy efficiency (HO501); proactive action on empty properties
- priority in rural areas for affordable housing for those wishing to become or remain part of the rural economy; planning process eased to allow low-impact and small scale rural living and working enterprises (Spring 99 conf).

© Green Party of England and Wales

Cry the beloved countryside

A requiem for England

Since I first travelled the English countryside 25 years ago, eyesores have become the norm. Drive up the coastline of Lincolnshire or east Kent, meander across Middle England from Worcester to Nottingham, survey modern Hertfordshire or south Lancashire and you will see some of the most depressing, anarchic development in western Europe. 'The finest crop that a field can grow /Is a hundred houses, all in a row.'

We are now witnessing what planners term the 'donutting' of England. By encouraging such services as supermarkets, leisure centres and business parks on the outskirts of towns, planners are turning suburbs inside out. This means that every journey to work, school or shop requires a car. Roads congest and the cost of public services rises. Meanwhile, town centres degenerate and are impoverished. The impact of donutting is most fierce in cities such as Bristol, Portsmouth, Leicester or Nottingham, where new out-of-town activities have been encouraged to replace dying inner-city ones.

We are not powerless. There is no 'planning necessity' for a single acre of green Britain to be consumed for building. Planning is what the nation decides. Although the much-quoted projected figure of 4.4 million new households required over 25 years (1991-2016) is now 3.8 million (for the dates 1996-2021), it is still a massive number. The Government policy on roads is that the existing stock can meet national pressure. Why not housing?

Unless Britain can use planning to revive 'the culture of the town', the breakneck suburbanisation of the country will continue

---

New building is consuming each year an area of countryside that is the size of Bristol (100sq km). Yet, according to the Council for the Protection of Rural England, six

times that amount of land is lying unused in towns and cities. How can ministers claim that building on greenbelt land is essential? It may be profitable to build afresh in green fields for future homeowners – but sensible planning reuses urban land and builds to higher densities where existing services are in place and traffic costs minimised. This may increase property prices.

Nor is it a matter of equity. Britain is one of Europe's most densely populated countries, yet it has the least densely populated towns and cities. Unless Britain can use planning to revive 'the culture of the town', the breakneck suburbanisation of the country will continue.

Protecting the environment has a cost. But greenfield development is not a 'necessity'.

- The above is an extract from the online version of the magazine *Country Life*, which is produced by IPC Media Ltd. The online magazine can be found at www.countrylife.co.uk

© IPC Media Ltd

How to campaign on supermarket developments

Retail impact: the effect of supermarket development on existing town centres

The effect of a superstore on an existing town centre is referred to as the retail impact. This article gives some background information on these effects as well as explaining current Government policy and why this is an important issue for local campaigners. There is also an explanation of retail impact studies and a guide to criticising those studies produced by the supermarket's consultants.

National trends on supermarket expansion

The most recent national figures show that the trend towards fewer, larger stores and edge- and out-of-town supermarkets is continuing. A recent study by the retail consultants Verdict found that the number of superstores will grow by 25 per cent during the next five years.

National policy on retail impact

The Government has set out how local authorities should assess retail proposals, and you can check that your Council is doing so. The matters to be taken into account where proposals are outside of existing town centres are:

- The impact on the development plan strategy
- The impact on the vitality and viability of existing centres (see below)
- Accessibility – new development should be located where a significant proportion of customers and staff will be able to get to the development by means other than car.

The likely cumulative effect of recently completed retail developments and outstanding planning permissions should also be taken into account when assessing the impact of a proposal.

Until July 1996 Government advice to Local Councils was that planning permission for retail development should not be refused on the grounds of retail impact 'unless there was clear evidence to suggest that the result would be to undermine the vitality and viability of a centre, which would otherwise continue to serve the community well'. This put great stress on the assessment of retail impact. The new Planning Policy Guidance 6 (PPG6) will reduce the weight attached to retail impact studies by placing greater emphasis on the overall impact on travel patterns.

Why are town centres important?

Town centres are part of our national and civic heritage. They can provide a focus for civic pride and a sense of place and local identity. They contain many of the public cultural assets like museums, libraries, attractive or distinctive townscape, and public squares and gardens. They play a significant role in the social life of the community as people who visit the centre for a variety of purposes meet and talk in the street. This engenders a sense of belonging to a place and community.

Protecting town centres also promotes sustainable development. They are easily served by public transport, and because many activities are concentrated in the one place, one trip can serve many purposes. Town centres facilitate competition because you can compare prices and goods in different shops easily. In contrast, to buy something expensive from an out-of-town store might involve trips backwards and forwards across town to compare the goods of several such stores.

Town centres are also important because they are accessible to all and not just to those with cars. Nationally about 33.3% of households do not own cars. Many of these people are elderly and find walking long distances and carrying shopping difficult. Many more people, particularly women with young children cannot use their car during the day, when their husbands are using it to get to work.

The language used in describing the functions and value of town centres is often abstract and can appear to have little to do with your experience. This is because 'experts' find it as difficult as you do to explain what goes on in town centres. If you can explain yourself more directly you will be doing everyone a favour.

Many towns grew up as markets at crossroads where the largest number of people could get to. In time, people offering other services and making goods would go there to take advantage of the people already there. Much later, employers who required large workforces would locate in town centres because they could draw on a larger pool of potential labour. These employees would spend money in shops further strengthening the town centre. This inter-dependence of activities is the key to the vitality and viability of town centres. Retailing nevertheless continues to underpin the success of town centres – most people go there to shop.

In many smaller market towns, the supermarket has become the main reason why most people go to town centres. Other reasons for visiting have been progressively withdrawn from many centres. Work is now dispersed to peripheral estates, or concentrated in larger towns. Banks are closing smaller branches. Gas and electricity bills are paid direct or by post and Government or Local Authorities are centralising their offices in larger towns. If trade is withdrawn from the town-centre supermarket to a new out-of-town store, other shops will close because they rely for their own trade on people who shop at the supermarket. This can have a 'snowball' effect, leading to further shop closures and undermining the whole social function of the centre.

Assessing the vitality and viability of your town centre

The impact of a new out-of-town supermarket proposal will depend on the vitality and viability of the town centre. The Government has identified certain key indicators of vitality and viability. In general, if it is shown that the existing town centre is both vital and viable – the supermarket applicant will be able to argue more easily that the development should go ahead.

- Diversity of uses – i.e. what other attractions are there to bring people to the centre? Examples include offices, pubs, cafes, housing in the centre, colleges, tourist attractions.
- Retailer representation – does the town have a good range of well known chain stores? Are numbers increasing or decreasing, and are there retailers wanting shops in the town?
- Rents – are shop rents in the main shopping area low compared with nearby towns? Are rents going up or down?
- Vacant shops – distinguishing between the main and secondary shopping frontages. A high proportion of vacancies, say above 10% in the main shopping area, is a sign of weak trading. But beware, even healthy centres have high vacancy levels at times of economic recession.
- Commercial yields – that is the capital value in relation to the expected market rent. Low yields indicate investor confidence. Unless you have the help of a commercial estate agent you will probably not be able to find out much information on commercial yields, but distrust simple figures put forward on behalf of the applicants. In many small towns, there are not enough recent transactions to indicate a representative yield.

- Pedestrian flows – obviously the more people there are on the street the more successful the centre. But the information must be collected on a consistent basis, and is only really valuable when it can be compared with flows elsewhere, or with previous counts in the same centre.
- Accessibility – is it easy to get to and around the town centre? Is there enough car parking that people will use? Are there plenty of buses?
- Customer views and behaviour – surveys can indicate what people think about their town centre. Strong dissatisfaction indicates a weak centre, but surprisingly, most people interviewed will say they are satisfied with any town centre unless they are asked about specific characteristics. Crime and the perception of safety in the street and in car parks are often significant.
- Environmental quality of the town centre – this includes not only appearance but noise, through traffic and air quality. Basically is it a nice place to be?

Local Authorities are requested to monitor the health of their town centres and you may be able to find out a lot of information on the centre from them. Ask if they have carried out a health check or have any reports on the town centre. There is generally no reason why these reports should be confidential. You have a legal right to see them if the Authority intends to rely on them in making reports to their Committees for instance on planning application or local plan proposals.

Retail impact studies

Retail impact studies aim to identify the likely trade diversion from existing centres, and to assess what this would mean to those centres. There is nothing clever or sophisticated in these studies. In fact they are poorly underpinned by any economic theory, and suffer from a dearth of information about both retail operations and shopping behaviour. Nevertheless, they are often the only evidence available. Because of their inherent weaknesses, planning decisions are not likely to turn on the precise calculations, but impact studies will be regarded as giving a general indication of the likely scale of impact. You should therefore concentrate criticism on major matters and not quibble when the broad conclusion would be the same.

Retail impact studies do vary, but the following stages are almost universally used in one form or another:

1. The definition of the catchment area

2. The estimation of catchment area expenditure
3. Town centre turnover
4. New store turnover
5. Assignment of new store turnover to existing centres
6. Assessment of impact on these centres

These stages are considered in more detail below:

1. The definition of the catchment area – commonly taken as the area within a 10- or 15-minute drive time, depending on the character of the area and the location of nearby towns. It is rarely based on survey evidence even where surveys are carried out. It is often overestimated – which means that it appears that expenditure is 'leaking' to other centres. This can then be claimed as 'clawback' to the centre, and reduces the amount of the new stores' turnover that has to be assessed as coming from the existing town centre.

2. Catchment area expenditure – calculated as the population of the catchment area multiplied by an estimate of retail expenditure per head. Estimates of local expenditure are available from various data consultancies. These are based on national rates in 1991 corrected for the social composition of the catchment area. The question that usually arises in relation to this exercise is what allowance should be made for increases in expenditure per head between 1991 and the first full year the store will open? Expenditure on food and everyday items (convenience goods) is increasing slowly – by about 0.4% a year. Expenditure on other goods (termed comparison goods) is growing much faster (about 3.5% a year). Foodstores are classified as convenience businesses, and expenditure through superstores is increasing faster than expenditure on convenience goods as they expand the range of goods they sell. Many applicants use business-based forecasts since this increases the expenditure apparently available. They shouldn't. Many inspectors at planning appeal inquiries will be familiar with the arguments even if you are not.

3. Town centre turnover – there is no good information on the turnover of town centres, or of individual shops. Commonly, the results of household surveys are used to apportion the catchment area expenditure to town centres. This is over-simplistic, the errors arising from sampling are large, and the estimate is dependent on the accurate definition of the catchment area. If the catchment area defined in the study is too large, the turnover of the town centre will also be over-estimated. Retail impact studies often do not explain how the town centre turnover has been estimated. It is always worth investigating – sometimes 'average' figures are used (often £250 per sq ft multiplied by the estimated sales floorspace). Sometimes a higher figure based on 'observation' is used, and a claim made that the centre is 'overtrading'.

Overtrading is jargon which means stores are trading better than average; it does not necessarily mean that the shops are crowded, and so does not provide justification for a new superstore.

Examine claims closely for real evidence, usually it is missing.

4. New store turnover – usually calculated on the basis of a figure of average turnover per sq ft of sales floorspace (i.e. Excluding storage offices etc.) for the major companies. Some information is available from published sources; it is calculated from the companies' annual reports, and varies according to how the reports are presented. To be consistent with other information used, particularly expenditure estimates, it should include VAT. It should not include petrol sales, which are now very significant for some companies. It is known that the performance of individual stores within a company varies very considerably – up to 50% of both sides of the average is often quoted. If the developer argues that this particular store will operate below average – and they may well do this to provide favourable retail and traffic impact studies – demand evidence as to why.

5. Assignment of new store turnover as trade diversion from existing centres – having calculated the turnover of the new store, it is necessary to estimate which centres and shops this will come from. This can be done using the results of the household survey and assuming that trade will be drawn in proportion to the way that money is spent now. Many people will say that more money is likely to be drawn from the other large foodstores in the area than survey results show, because they are in most direct competition. There is some justice in this claim, although survey results will usually also lead to the same conclusion. Very often a 'judgmental' approach is used. This means that it has been made up to look plausible, and that there is no supporting evidence. Point out to the council, or the Inspector at an inquiry, that they are entitled to know how the trade diversion figures have been calculated and to examine each assumption that has been made, if they are going to rely on the applicant's conclusions.

6. Impact – the trade diversion for the centre is calculated as a percentage of the centre's estimated turnover. Convenience and comparison turnover are usually considered separately. If any of the above stages are seriously flawed, the impact figure is obviously meaningless. Try to assess whether correction would increase or decrease the impact figure. There is no set level above which impact is regarded as significant. Much depends on the vitality and viability of the centre, and the impact figure should be assessed against the indicators described in this brief. However, for food stores the diversion of between 10% and 15% of a centre's convenience turnover have been considered as significant by Inspectors. Above 20% will almost always be.

Retail impact studies are not sophisticated and not produced by 'experts'. Anyone with a calculator and patience should be able to sit down, work through it, and come to the same conclusions on the basis of the same assumptions. Otherwise it is not good evidence. Assess the assumptions, are they logical? Are they reasonable as a matter of judgement? What evidence is there to support them? Above all, remember that if people want you to believe them, they must be able to justify their study with hard evidence.
© *Sustain*

Fighting urban sprawl

Information from Friends of the Earth

The Department of the Environment predicts that the number of households in England will grow by 4.4 million over 25 years (or until 2016). All these households will need somewhere to live. There is now pressure for massive new house building – much of it urban sprawl on greenfield sites.

All these new houses in the countryside generate huge amounts of new traffic. The housing crisis is now the most serious threat to a sustainable transport system in the country. What's more, house building has enormous impacts on energy use, water supply, mineral extraction, soils, landscape and wildlife.

- The Government sets 'targets' for regions to build houses – the 'predict and provide' approach. These figures bear little or no relationship to local environmental considerations.
- The Government accepts that this demand for housing, 'if met in the simplest way – using greenfield sites – would result in wholly unacceptable environmental damage'. However, current policies encourage greenfield development, and need radical revision.
- Since 1945 an area greater than the combined total of Greater London, Berkshire, Hertfordshire and Oxfordshire has been urbanised. The house builders want massive greenfield developments.
- Meanwhile, up to 800,000 houses in England lie empty, and a similar number of flats over shops could be brought into use. Acres of derelict land could be used, if we could find ways to clean it up.

We're calling for:

- Resistance to the centrally imposed Government housing targets. Local authorities should be encouraged to reject these targets, which take no account of local environmental conditions;
- Grassroots opposition to greenfield housing developments which damage the environment and generate new traffic;
- Tough targets to put new housing in urban areas, through filling empty homes and using derelict land;
- Urban regeneration with traffic reduction. In particular we need to see high quality, urban housing, with traffic calming and the reduction of parking levels.

Take action

- Help to support local shops and businesses, especially if you can walk or cycle to them.

Up to 800,000 houses in England lie empty, and a similar number of flats over shops could be brought into use. Acres of derelict land could be used, if we could find ways to clean it up

---

- Using the information here, write to your MP outlining your opposition to further greenfield housing development, and the need to make better use of empty homes.
- Get involved in opposing greenfield housing locally. You can get hold of our new guide to fighting greenfield housing – *Stopping the Sprawl*. Price £7.00 (incl. P&P) quote code L417 – from Publications Despatch, Friends of the Earth, 56 Alma Street, Luton LU1 2PH (with cheque, postal order or credit card details). Or call 020 7490 1555.
- Urge your local council to resist out-of-town developments of all types, and to resist impossible Government targets for house building.
- Join FOE local groups fighting to halt urban sprawl and aid urban regeneration in your area. Call 0990 22 44 88 for details.
- If you want a more in-depth look at housing in England have a look at the URGENT! website at www.urgent.org.uk

© Friends of the Earth

City rich prop up rural poor

Demand for farm properties sustains country life. By James Meikle

City slickers' dreams of living in the country are creating a new gold rush down on the farm – despite the worst rural recession since the 1930s.

Demands for top-notch historic farmhouses and their accompanying land is running so high that in some areas nearly half the would-be buyers have no farming background.

Self-made millionaires are joining middle-aged professionals, often with young children, in seeking an escape from the cities, with email and the internet helping them keep on the job during weekends.

Now land agents say that the demand is so great that there are not enough farms to go round. Owners of family farms in financial trouble and with no offspring interested in carrying on are still reluctant to give up their homes, while others who want to expand to survive by spreading their costs over larger acreage are having to compete with increasing numbers in the 'house and back garden' market.

Home seekers want attractive period properties with a bit of land which they can use to make a profit, often by leasing it to 'real' farmers next door. Turning farm cottages into holiday lets is also proving an attractive option.

The wave of farm buying by non-farmers followed earlier raids beyond the stockbroker belt in the home counties over the last 25 years. But eager buyers are now looking further afield. Parts of Yorkshire are also an attraction to the new rich from the northern cities, while Londoners' hopes of buying land in Norfolk are pushing prices sky high.

Knight Frank, a leading agent in the field, has even extended traditional home-selling hints to the farmyard, reminding farmers whose properties might attract the new townie breed to fill in potholes in the drives, tidy up tacky out-buildings, cut their lawns and steam clean dirty carpets.

James Crawford, of the company, said: 'These chores are the equivalent of polishing your shoes before going to an interview.'

Knight Frank has about 700 potential private buyers on the lookout for farms or estates over £1m and half of them are looking for homes rather than commercial operations. There are 22 farms and estates on the books at the moment.

Mr Crawford said: 'People can't find a house with 10 or 20 acres so they are looking at farms with 200-300 acres. It's very simple now to buy a farm and produce a bit of income and get pleasure without losing security.'

Ian Hepburn, a partner in the Salisbury office of Strutton & Parker, said people coming out of London often aspired to a classical Georgian rectory in a few acres. 'That costs in general £1m or over nowadays but an average 100-to 150-acre dairy farm

---

Home seekers want attractive period properties with a bit of land which they can use to make a profit, often by leasing it to 'real' farmers next door

---

at the moment is going for between £650,000 and £800,000. Sometimes people think "What am I going to do with all that land?" But in most cases those farmers who are soldiering on are looking for more land and are likely to be interested in a bit of contract farming or renting.

'But the house must be in the right position, preferably in the middle of its own land. If it is not beautiful, it must be on a site where it can be converted or enlarged. Ideally there needs to be a bit of rolling countryside or a couple of woods.

'Not all ex-dairy farms are going to be bought up – especially if they are low lying, with a grim farmhouse and tired old buildings.'

Mr Hepburn said: 'The people coming in want to be in the country, and the money from these non-farming buyers is helping to sustain the agricultural economy.'

Justin Marking, head of the agricultural agency of FPD Savills, said the demand for good properties as homes was putting 16% to 30% extra on prices. 'Over 40% of our farm buyers to the west of London last year were from outside agriculture. Three years ago it was one in five.

'We are finding major players with their own businesses are now prepared to work from home as communications get better.

© Guardian Newspapers Limited, 2000

26

The housing crisis is not just an urban phenomenon

By Derek Brown

There are plenty of delightful places to live in rural Britain, as anyone knows who has flicked the pages of *Country Life* magazine. But it is a bitter irony of modern rural life that many of those born and brought up in the countryside can least afford to live there.

Far from being a distinctively urban phenomenon, homelessness is a widespread and spreading scourge in the countryside. And although the extent and the causes of it vary hugely from region to region, there are factors common to all:

- A surge of demand by city-dwellers for a permanent or 'weekend' home in the country has driven up prices and rents.
- A desperate lack of development land in the more sought-after areas has further boosted the value of existing properties.
- Incomes from rural employment, especially but not exclusively agriculture, are well below the national average.
- The continuing system of 'tied' dwellings, in which accommodation is part of a low-wage employment package, means that when the job goes or the worker retires, he or she is without a home or the means to acquire one.

Quantifying the problem is as difficult as defining it. To some people, the countryside means remoteness, even wildness. To others, it is embodied in village greens and quaint cottages. The campaigning group Action With Communities in Rural England takes the view that all non-urban areas are by definition rural. By that definition, there are 11m people living today in rural England and, shockingly, an estimated 25% of them live below the official poverty line.

The Countryside Alliance, noted more for its defence of bloodsports than its support of the rural poor, estimates that rural house prices are now 10-15% higher than the national average. (That again disguises huge regional disparities, but it is indisputably true that a character-cottage in a commuter village is worth a good deal more than a suburban house of equivalent size in the city.)

The issue of rural housing is bedevilled by conflicting interests. The demand for new affordable homes is often most bitterly resisted by newcomers to an area who feel that 'their' peace and tranquillity is threatened. (The same sort of people regularly incur the scorn of country folk by complaining that farming is smelly, or noisy, or both.)

With local authorities no longer building homes, much of the miserably inadequate new stock is being provided by housing associations and, of course, by private builders happy to make a buck from the craze for country dwelling. Both are regularly thwarted by Green Belt regulations and other planning requirements.

The CPRE (the Campaign for the Protection of Rural England) strongly supports the planning laws, and believes they are under threat, especially in the crowded south-east, where the government wants 1.1 million new homes by 2016. That target, says CPRE assistant director Tony Burton, implies a nightmare future of sprawl and congestion, in a region already at bursting point. 'Building over one million homes would shatter the Green Belt, intrude on land protected for its landscape or wildlife value, and lose valuable farmland,' he says.

Many campaigners, for the homeless as well as for the countryside, are outraged that little is being done to regenerate the 560 square kilometres – the government's own figure, recorded in last year's Land Use Database – of decayed urban land. Those 'brownfield' areas could sprout up to three-quarters of a million new homes, and leave huge swaths of countryside free to sprout more natural crops.

© *Guardian Newspapers Limited, 2000*

The rural revolution

Revealed, secret plan to bring in a tourist tax and encourage farmers to build on prime land

By Adam Powell

Prime farmland should be freed for development and a tourism tax imposed on visitors to rural beauty spots, says a secret report to the Government on the future of the countryside.

The leaked document by Cabinet Office mandarins contains proposals for a revolution in rural Britain. Other proposals include VAT on new homes and rural 'park and ride' schemes.

Farmers would be encouraged to cash in on the growing tourism and leisure industry by building holiday homes on farmland, ending reliance on agricultural incomes and subsidies.

The report from the Performance and Innovation Unit – set up by Mr Blair two years ago – was ordered by Tony Blair and is supposed to be released in six weeks.

But its contents are so explosive that publication might be shelved altogether, especially in light of the tensions over farming and the threats to the traditional rural way of life. Some of the findings will, however, go towards the Government's rural White Paper which is due for release from John Prescott's Department of the Environment, Transport and the Regions next spring.

The most far-reaching proposal is to end the planning restrictions on prime farmland which has been protected as a national asset for centuries.

It will open the way for farmers to sell up to developers or themselves to build new homes or even 'model villages'.

The Government would encourage such entrepreneurial ideas and opportunities as part of a move away from sole reliance on farming and agriculture.

The report, described as a 'rural audit', outlines a vision of a new 'living countryside' with market towns at the centre of a vibrant reborn rural as opposed to agricultural economy.

The reforms to the Common Agricultural Policy being pushed through in Europe will also encourage farmers to move towards more diverse businesses. The VAT proposal could add 17.5 per cent to the price of the 150,000 new houses and flats sold every year, most of them in the suburbs or on greenfield sites at the edge of towns and cities.

Revenue could come in too from tolls on country lanes, or by introducing 'park and ride' schemes in busy tourist areas

The levy would go alongside the imposition of full planning controls on agricultural land to balance the effects of releasing it for development.

The Agriculture Ministry has a veto over allowing farm land to be built on, which is hampering the Environment Department's plan to build four million homes over the next 16 years. Farmers stand to make a fortune.

But their land and buildings would be governed by the same laws that control development in towns and cities.

If the proposals are backed by the Government, they could herald a new era of prosperity in some parts of the country, especially the South East, where farmers could become overnight millionaires by selling their land or developing it.

Mr Prescott has recently begun to backtrack on his target of 60 per cent for brownfield building, and is instead looking at encouraging large-scale new developments on rural land in the South East.

Other sources of income for the Treasury could come from a tourism tax in 'honeypot' areas such as the Cotswolds or the Peak District. Such areas could introduce tourist taxes, possibly surcharges on hotel and guest house bills. But the unit also suggests holidaymakers could be invited to tick boxes on restaurant and hotel bills to declare their status as tourists. They would then be charged extra as a voluntary 'congestion tax' on anything from a cup of tea upwards.

This, the report believes, could pay for the damage caused by too many tourists and persuade them to visit other areas.

To improve transport, it suggests there should be state-subsidised taxis to take young country people to work.

Firms should also set up car pools so employees could book a vehicle when they needed one. Revenue could come in too from tolls on country lanes, or by introducing 'park and ride' schemes in busy tourist areas.

Farmers and landowners have reacted furiously to the leaked details, saying the lifting of restrictions on farmland could see a national resource squandered.

© *The Daily Mail*
October, 1999

People and houses and the countryside

A hot topic in the UK over the next few years will be the provision of houses. This is particularly highlighted in south-east England where Government-sponsored research has predicted a massive rise in building rate with much of it in the open countryside – in what are called 'greenfield sites'. The following are two contributions to the debate, the first is an extract from CPRW's Branch Bulletin (No. 61) and the second is a follow-up article by Professor Arthur Thomasson, Chairman of the Pembrokeshire Branch. Both of them, in fact, are calls to action to address what is potentially a great threat to the loss of countryside in certain key areas of pressure.

Housing and greenfield sites

In most parts of Wales the main generator of countryside loss is the allocation of greenfield land for housing. Planning authorities are revising their development plans and setting new housing targets for up to 2016. The authorities are now permitted to set their own targets, which used to be imposed on them by the former Welsh Office.

The main reason for the need for new housing is due to the continuing evolution of smaller average family size – and of this the largest single group is single-person households. This must mean that there is a significant local need – i.e. a need by existing local population. Therefore a large part of the authority's need must be for smaller homes.

Most planning authorities have traditionally allocated housing land and then allowed the house-building industry to decide what homes should be built. This approach seems to lead to developers preferring to build quite large, low-density houses on greenfield sites. Houses that are frequently taken by the retired and commuters – people often moving from outside the area.

The Government now wants 60% of housing to be sited on brownfield land (already developed land) but many authorities in Wales do not have useful amounts of such land. Certainly it seems wrong to provide for new housing in a way that is unlikely to satisfy the 'local need' and it seems wrong to be using greenfield sites to encourage commuting. Branches are encouraged to study these aspects in their area's emerging Unitary Development Plans and to strongly promote the planning of housing for identified 'local needs' on brownfield land. It would also help if branches liaised with Head Office so that we can make any necessary representations to the National Assembly.

. . . and the builders agree

The House Builders' Federation have themselves launched a campaign 'Old Land, New Houses' with a threefold aim:

- To show the commitment of the industry to the development of recycled land;
- To highlight the difficulties house builders experience developing recycled land and to promote solutions;
- To encourage the public to participate in the process of identifying sites of recycled land.

The Federation is asking members of the public to let it have details of any previously-used land that might be used for housing. The considerations that the public is asked to take into account are the size of the site, whether it is easily accessible, its previous use and, more import-antly, whether it could become an area that would be an attractive place to live. A hot-line is open for calls – the number is 020 7608 5107.

Further details of this campaign will be sent on request.

• The above is an extract from the magazine *Rural Wales*, which is produced by the Council for the Protection of Rural Wales (CPRW). See page 41 for address details.

© *Council for the Protection of Rural Wales (CPRW)*
Spring, 2000

Coastline of sand and cement

Information from the National Farmers' Union (NFU)

Over 230 miles of Britain's coastline have disappeared under concrete in the past 35 years, according to a study commissioned by the National Trust. The study's author, Dr John Whittow, warned that many more stretches of coastline would be lost to development – mainly housing – unless urgent action was taken by national and local government.

Dr Whittow, a retired landscape evolution expert at Reading University, said: 'It was quite shocking to discover how much of the natural coast we have lost.' The study is updating an earlier one, previously conducted by the university's geography department in 1965. North Wales was the worst hit, with Flint losing 44 per cent and Denbigh 36 per cent of its coastal land. Dr Whittow said housing sprawl had left Denbigh with just 'a few hundred yards of natural coast'.

Somerset has suffered badly too, with 20 per cent of its coastline disappearing under concrete since 1970, mainly because of industry at Avonmouth, Hinkley Point power station and 'sprawl' between Burnham-on-Sea and Clevedon. Other serious losses have occurred in Co. Durham (21.6 per cent), Norfolk (10.5 per cent) and Suffolk (7.5 per cent).

The research shows that five per cent of the coastline has been lost in the whole of South-west England and nearly six per cent in East Anglia. In the North-east the figure is 9.5 per cent and in Wales seven per cent.

Houses and industry had covered most of the 'lost' coast. The introduction of designated protected areas had increased protection for some stretches of coastline, but may have left other areas, unprotected by designation, vulnerable and under pressure. Local planning authorities are being urged to hold back the tide of development and the National Trust, which looks after 600 miles of coast in England, Wales and Northern Ireland, is being called upon to increase its efforts to buy and safeguard coastal land.

The original survey in 1965 prompted the Trust to launch the Enterprise Neptune Campaign aimed at identifying underdeveloped coastal areas worthy of protection. The new survey shows that a total of around 235 miles of coast have been developed in the past three decades. Countryside campaigning groups say Britain's coastline is as important as other areas of natural interest, and it should be protected for ecological as well as heritage reasons.

Some land has been gained, mainly through the decommissioning of Ministry of Defence land and the decline of quarrying and mining industries. However Dr Whittow warned that more vigilance was needed. 'The gains are encouraging but very small compared to the losses. We have to guard against the less scrupulous developers who will exploit any weakness shown by the planning authorities.'

A spokesman for the Trust said: 'The study shows how easy it is to lose coastline. Our campaign to protect these beautiful areas goes on but it is crucial that we have the support of local and central government.'

• The above is an extract from *Rural News*, the magazine produced by the National Farmers' Union. See their web site for details at www.nfucountryside.org.uk

© National Farmers' Union

Meacher announces better protection for countryside

More than five million acres of Britain's most beautiful countryside will have better protection from development following a Government amendment to the Countryside and Rights of Way Bill.

This is a victory for the campaign to get better protection for Areas of Outstanding Natural Beauty (AONBs), an issue championed by the Ramblers. Michael Meacher, Minister for the Environment, announced that AONBs will be treated as though they were National Parks for planning purposes.

Until now AONBs have, in theory, been afforded the same landscape value as National Parks but have not been given the planning protection that they have needed. National Parks are controlled by a National Park Authority (NPA) which takes planning decisions in the interest of the park in order to conserve and enhance its natural beauty, wildlife and cultural heritage, and to promote opportunities for public understanding and enjoyment of its special qualities. Planning guidance states that major development should not take place in National Parks and all such developments must be subject to the most rigorous examination.

Although the announcement does not mean that AONBs will now get their own special kind of planning board, it does mean that local authorities will be more accountable for their protection from development. Included in the announcement was the requirement for local authorities to adopt a management plan for each AONB. This should provide a clear starting point for a comprehensive strategy for AONBs and allow more thought to be given to the purpose of the area and its enhancement.

Given the current pressure for development, particularly in the south-east, this is a welcome move to secure the future protection of some of our most beautiful pieces of countryside.

© Ramblers' Association

Developers getting the green message

Information from the Countryside Agency

When building takes place in or near to the countryside, how do you get developers to minimise its impact on the community and compensate for any loss of green space and enjoyment?

Research for the Countryside Agency has shown that, although many local authorities remain wary of 'planning gain', a growing number expect developers to contribute towards greening their developments and the surrounding countryside.

Using planning obligations (often known as Section 106 agreements), local authorities have negotiated developers' contributions to woodland planting, new cycleways and footpaths, country parks, nature reserves, and new village facilities.

To encourage more planners to follow suit, the research study gives 44 examples of benefits to the countryside from developers' contributions.

One example is part of the Coulby Newham development, a major homes scheme comprising 19 housing sites and forming a neighbourhood on the southern fringe of Middlesbrough, south of the A174.

Here private house-builders and housing associations have helped pay for specific features that bring countryside benefits.
They include:
- planting new trees
- protecting hedgerows
- creating new footpaths and cycleways linking the housing with the neighbourhood park and nature reserve
- developing a countryside centre/ community centre
- helping to pay for a neighbourhood park and to maintain a nearby nature reserve.

Tony Duggan, development manager with the borough council, said: 'Middlesbrough is such a built-up area it was important for us to "green" as much as we could, and the council made it a high priority to protect and enhance the limited area of countryside that was available.

'These specific contributions have made big improvements to the residents' surroundings, raising their quality of life and adding to the attractiveness of the area for those seeking to buy.'

Detailed planning permission was granted in February 1995, and construction began that summer. The majority of the houses are now occupied.

The funding from the developers at Coulby Newham ran into hundreds of thousands of pounds and, through the development of the countryside centre, the borough council has been able to expand its training and volunteer work. The centre will also be a gateway for visitors to the Tees Forest.

Tony said: 'In the past, housing developers were interested primarily in profit from building new homes and often paid only lip service to the landscape areas outside the estates they built.

'To some extent, many councils let developers off the hook by allowing them to destroy existing landscape areas and replace them with small areas of public open space of virtually no benefit.'

The benefits pledged by the developers at Coulby Newham were seen as an intrinsic part of the development process, not an add-on. Since Middlesbrough Borough Council owned the land, it was able to specify environmental benefits as

---

'They need to have in place a green context for development'

---

part of the legal agreement for sale of land to the developer, as well as making a Section 106 agreement as part of the planning process.

The developers were expected to include outline layout and indicative landscape schemes in their preliminary submissions — to avoid landscape issues going to the bottom of the list and becoming marginalised in later stages of development.

Jeremy Worth, head of planning at the Countryside Agency, said: 'You don't have to own the land to make a scheme like this work. Coulby Newham is a good example of what can be done by local authorities throughout England, and there is every reason for them to make similar agreements with developers elsewhere.

'But an important message to emerge from our research is that local authorities need to include these issues in their development plans, backed up by other strategies for nature conservation, greenways, woodland planting and other environmental benefits.

'They need to have in place a green context for development, putting the right plans and policy framework in place at the outset to show developers what they expect of them and why. When that happens, everyone stands to be a winner.'

- *Countryside Benefits from Developer Contributions* (price £15 plus £2.50 p&p) is available from the School of Planning, Oxford Brookes University, tel. 01865 483491. Countryside Agency advice based on the report will be sent to all planning authorities later this year.

- The above information is an extract from the Countryside Agency's web site which can be found at www.countryside.gov.uk

© The Countryside Agency

The state of the countryside 2000

A summary of key facts

The British love affair with the countryside is continuing. 50% of people say they would like to live in the countryside, with 84% concerned about things that may happen to it. But according to a new report published today (26 April) by the government's statutory advisers, the Countryside Agency, behind this picture is a more complex story.

Ewen Cameron, chairman of the Countryside Agency, said: 'The facts speak for themselves. Some people in the countryside may enjoy the "good life" but others suffer exclusion and isolation. Behind the rosy image of the rural idyll lie some very real problems of rural isolation, a declining environment, pressurised and declining services and a vulnerable rural economy. Disadvantage can be hard to uncover because it is often masked by the proximity of affluence.'

The report shows that England's rural communities are going through a period of great change. Mr Cameron said: 'Some of the things people most value about life in the countryside are being eroded – and that is worrying them. There is an unsettling fear that villages and market towns are losing their sense of community, as well as the relative security and freedom from crime which many have enjoyed for a long time. Average weekly wages are lowest in rural counties such as Cornwall, Northumberland and Shropshire. To make matters worse, many essential rural services are either closing or face the threat of closure, which creates particular problems for the less well-off trying to get basic services if their post office, doctor's surgery or village shop has disappeared.'

Mr Cameron said: 'At the same time, the countryside is changing. It is evolving alongside the rest of modern Britain – new job opportunities are being created by IT and other modern businesses. We have seen a radical government review of countryside policy and look forward to developing new initia-

> ' . . . the countryside is changing. It is evolving alongside the rest of modern Britain – new job opportunities are being created by IT and other modern businesses

tives, such as help for market towns. Our overall aim is sustainable development in the countryside to ensure a living countryside for future generations.'

He concluded: 'This report is more than an encyclopaedia of facts. It is a valuable tool, and sets out the challenges which face the government in their forthcoming Rural White Paper. Equipped with well-researched data, we can take informed action to reduce undesirable changes taking place in the countryside. It should be used by all of us with an interest in the welfare of the English countryside to inform our actions and policies.'

Highlights from the *State of the Countryside 2000* report include:

- 50% of British people said they would like to live in the countryside
- 84% expressed concern about things that may happen to the countryside
- one in five people (23%) live in rural England, growing faster (10.3%) than in England as a whole (5.3%) between 1994 and 1998
- 13,148 settlements in rural England have populations of less than 500

- YOU CAN VISIT OUR WEB SITE...

- total farm income has fallen to its lowest level since entering the Common Agricultural Policy
- hidden unemployment is higher in rural areas (16.3%). A higher proportion of rural people are dependent on part-time work (26.4%) and seasonal jobs
- low income – the lowest weekly wages are in Cornwall (£297), Northumberland (£315), Isle of Wight (£323) and Shropshire (£339) (cf. England £405)
- traffic is increasing faster on rural roads than elsewhere yet car ownership is essential. Rural people often have no choice of public transport. Low-income rural households are twice as likely to run a car as similar urban households
- vehicle-related thefts are up 24% in rural areas compared to 10% in inner cities
- rural homelessness is increasing – between 1992 and 1996 it rose from 11.8% to 14.4%
- areas designated in order to protect high-quality habitats and particular species have increased appreciably but biodiversity in the countryside continues to decline steeply
- 2.2 million tonnes of soil per year are lost from a total of 26,300 sq km of arable land in England through erosion by water

Public concern for the countryside

Social attitudes reveal a high level of public concern for the countryside. Of the people questioned in the 1999 British Social Attitudes Survey:

88% agreed that 'industry should be prevented from causing damage to the countryside, even if this sometimes leads to higher prices' — 88%

84% expressed concern 'about things that may happen to the countryside' — 84%

80% agreed that is was 'more important to keep green-belt areas than to build new homes there' — 80%

75% considered 'the countryside should be protected from development' — 75%

73% agreed that 'new housing should be built in cities, towns and villages rather than in the countryside' — 73%

69% felt that 'modern methods of farming have caused damage to the countryside' — 69%

50% would 'like to live in the countryside' — 50%

Source: The State of the Countryside 2000

- land in organic farming has increased and now accounts for 1.3% of agricultural land-demand for organic food is increasing at 40% per year, supply at only 25% per year
- 450,000 hectares are now in Community Forests within easy reach of 50% of England's population. More than one thousand hectares of derelict, urban-fringe land have been reclaimed
- there are an estimated 169,000 km of public rights of way, including some 3,000km on ten national trails in England.

The State of the Countryside 2000 report gives an overview of rural facts and trends and urban comparisons, and explores how people view the countryside. Information is drawn from many sources.

The report is available free from Countryside Agency Publications, P.O. Box 125, Wetherby, West Yorkshire LS23 7EP Tel 0870 120 6466. A set of accompanying regional reports will be published later this year. Alternatively, see their web site at www.countryside.gov.uk

© The Countryside Agency

Rural problems

Country dwellers worry more about housing, jobs and transport than crime, says report

By James Meikle

Most people in the countryside do not think rural crime is a problem despite the furore surrounding the jailing of farmer Tony Martin, the head of the government's main rural quango for England said yesterday.

Ewen Cameron, said they were more worried by shortages of jobs, housing, transport, shops, banking and other services, even if some did suffer the 'unsettling fear' that villages and market towns were losing the 'relative security and freedom from crime which many have enjoyed for a long time'.

Mr Cameron, chairman of the Countryside Agency, conceded that countryside crime was increasing 'from very low levels' and supported the idea that police should introduce target times to respond to emergencies instead of simply supplying more 'bobbies on the beat'. But crime 'does not seem to me a real problem in rural communities. There is a fear of crime but there are many other greater problems that rural communities have to deal with.'

The agency's annual report on the state of the countryside reinforced the message that 'absolute risks of crime in rural districts are in most respects lower than in most urban areas'. In 1995 3.9% of rural households were burgled compared with 6.3% in urban areas and 10.3% in inner cities. People living in rural areas felt safer on their streets and public confidence in the police was higher in rural areas.

However, some types of crime had increased in rural areas at a rate greater than elsewhere. Thefts of and from cars, vans and lorries went up by 24% in rural areas between 1991 and 1995 compared with 4% in urban areas and 10% in inner cities. In the same period, muggings and other 'contact' crime had risen by 60% in the countryside, 48% in urban areas and 91% in inner cities. In addition, fear of burglary or armed robbery had been a factor in the closure of rural post offices.

The report noted evidence that people in rural areas felt more vulnerable to property crime committed by others from outside the local area. 'Fear of crime is exacerbated by community fragmentation and reduced social cohesion and awareness of increasingly stretched police resources and decreased scope for traditional policing methods.'

Mr Cameron was eager to play down the row over policing. He said the biggest problem in the countryside might be caused by the farming crisis. 'Virtually all the landscape in this country is man-made and related to agricultural management of the land.'

He suggested consumers held the fate of the countryside in their choices between home and imported produce.

'You can eat the view. Consumers ought to be eating the view.

'They ought to realise that if they love and cherish the countryside, their purchasing decisions very much affect this.'

While some people in the countryside did enjoy the good life, others suffered isolation. 'Behind the rural idyll lie some very real problems of rural isolation, a declining environment, pressurised and declining services and a vulnerable rural economy. Disadvantage can be hard to uncover because it is often masked by the proximity of affluence.'

Tim Yeo, the shadow agriculture minister, said: 'This report, from the government's own rural policy advisers, exposes Labour's blatant lie that there is no rural crisis. It reveals the deep-seated economic, social and environmental problems that face rural areas, many of which may result from Labour policy.'

The agency's verdict was grimmer than that presented by a cabinet office report to Tony Blair in February, which concluded that the countryside was 'prosperous, contented and reasonably well-served'. It noted that rural communities, traditionally perceived as being more cohesive, friendlier and safer than urban ones, were under threat from the increase in people commuting rather than working in the community, the loss of local culture, language and dialect and conflicts between incomers and locals and farmers.

© Guardian Newspapers Limited, 2000

Land under threat and protection

Vast areas of the countryside are being placed under unnecessary threat by local authorities seeking to attract new employment to their areas. Huge over-allocation of land is undermining attempts to promote an urban renaissance and tackle social exclusion. This is the claim by the Council for the Protection of Rural England, in a report published this week. *Towards Sustainable Economic Development* highlights major weaknesses in current approaches to planning for employment-related development.

Neil Sinden, CPRE's Head of Planning and Local Government, says, 'understandably, the desire to attract new jobs is often a top priority for local authorities. Yet, this can be achieved without the huge over-allocation of greenfield sites for business parks, offices and industry that now affects many parts of the country. A glut of greenfield sites makes it more difficult to steer economic investment to where it can tackle pockets of high unemployment, secure urban renewal and reduce the need to travel by car.'

According to the CPRE the report identifies a number of key weaknesses:

- Vague and inconsistent Government planning policies relating to economic development;
- Wasteful competition between local authorities to attract scarce investment;
- Mistaken assumptions that businesses will always prefer greenfield to previously developed sites; and
- Insufficient clarity over the need for Regional Development Agencies to operate within the framework provided by Regional Planning Guidance.

The report concludes that a radical review of planning for economic development at the national, regional and local levels is needed. Better protection of rural land should be seen as an opportunity to promote more sustainable development rather than as an obstacle to economic growth.

The future use of land is highlighted again this week at a Forum for the Application of Conservation Techniques Conference in Cambridge. Baroness Young of Old Scone, chairman of English Nature, will announce measures to help land managers deliver biodiversity targets. The package has been put together following a three-year partnership by conservation organisations, to tackle problems reconciling land management with conservation. Measures expected include:

- A Practical Solutions handbook outlining new techniques, machinery and ideas that can help protect wildlife;
- A Grazing Animals Project, to help farmers develop and maintain sustainable grazing schemes;
- and Machinery Rings, a scheme to make specialist machines more available for wildlife management work.

• The above is an extract from the National Farmers' Union web site www.nfucountryside.org.uk

© National Farmers' Union (NFU)

Loophole threatens our village greens

By Mark Rowe

Developers are exploiting an obscure legal loophole to destroy some of the last remaining village greens in England and cover them with bricks and concrete.

There are fears that up to 50 greens could disappear under housing as a result of a law that, bizarrely, punishes open spaces for attracting too many visitors. They include greens from Cambridge to Devon, and Hertfordshire to Lancashire, where one in the constituency of environment minister Michael Meacher is threatened.

The loophole is in the 1965 Commons Registration Act which insists that for an open space to qualify as a green, most people using it must live nearby. If too many people from outside this locality use the green – perhaps because it is an attractive place for picnicking or there is a popular pub close to it – the attempt will fail.

Villagers and locals wanting to register a green – a status which protects it from development – must present a map showing the land in question and the area within which the people using the green live. They need to show there is a recognisable community living close to the land. But with the spread of urban areas this is difficult to do.

The Leys Farm, for example, is a green struggling for survival in the urban sprawl that surrounds Blackpool, Lancashire. Songbirds once flourished among the wild flowers, trees and meadows.

But that was before the local authority gave planning permission for a new development of 120 houses on the land. Then the bulldozers moved in and now the trees, the hedgerows and the birds associated with the four-acre site have gone.

Local people in Blackpool are not giving up on Leys Farm without a fight. Six protesters are camping on what is left of the green, under threat of eviction. In a last desperate move they have submitted a new application to register the land as a green – and this time they think they have a copper-bottomed case.

'The first time the council got out the lawyers and QCs and threw out our application saying we hadn't defined the locality,' said Beverley Moy, leader of the campaign, who spends much of her time in a tent at the site, a mile north of Blackpool's beach and illuminations.

'It's very hard to define. Not many local people could say exactly which part of town their house falls into. With urban sprawl it's harder to do.

'This time we have defined the locality by the parish and we hope this will be enough to get a public inquiry. Leys Farm has been used by local people since the 1950s for all kinds of pastimes. It is the only natural piece of land left in Blackpool and it's been harrowing to see it destroyed.'

The local authority, Blackpool Borough Council, stands by its decision. David Owen, chairman of the council's development control committee, said: 'I know a town green when I see one and this is just rough land. This land hasn't reached the standard needed.'

Similar threats to greens are being encountered in Littleport, Cambridgeshire, where permission has been granted to build a health centre on recreational land, and the Ilsham Valley, in Torquay, where there is a proposal to build a pumping station.

Developers are planning a commercial football pitch in Mengham Park on Hayling Island, Hampshire, while development plans are threatening Spitalbrook Green in Hoddesdon, Hertfordshire. A green in Royton, Oldham, in environment minister Michael Meacher's constituency, is also under threat.

The Open Spaces Society says a new, unambiguous, definition of a village green must be enshrined in the new Countryside and Rights of Way Bill to avoid further development on open spaces.

Kate Ashbrook, the society's general secretary, said: 'Too many areas of open space are being threatened by the bulldozers. The law has to be changed so that you don't have to demonstrate that people live nearby.'

© The Independent
May, 2000

Villages suffering as new banks close scores of branches

By Ben Taylor

The massive cost to rural communities of the rush to turn building societies into banks was revealed yesterday.

Former societies which became public limited companies have closed nearly three times as many branches as they open.

A ruthless wave of cost-cutting has left scores of small towns and villages stranded without a single financial institution.

However, those societies which stood firm and chose to remain mutual continued to open more branches than they shut.

The news comes as thousands of rural post offices are threatened with closure because of Government plans to pay benefits directly into claimants' bank accounts.

At the same time, two-thirds of country parishes do not have a village shop, 83 per cent have no daily bus service, and nearly 50 per cent have no post office or school. Police patrols are increasingly provided by officers working miles from the villages they serve.

Yesterday's report on banks paints a startling picture of how 'demutualisation' has changed the face of the High Street. The trend, which started with the sell-off of the Abbey National in 1991, triggered a cash bonanza for millions in lucrative windfall payments as societies effectively bought out their members.

Often, savers were urged to vote for conversion to bank status through heavy advertising campaigns and massive leaflet drops.

Now a three-year study by experts at Newcastle University has revealed how many who gratefully accepted their one-off payments may have seen their local branch close for ever.

Figures for 1995 to 1998 show that building societies opened 242 branches and closed 227 – a net gain of 15 and maintaining a branch total of nearly 2,900.

But eight of their former colleagues – including the Halifax, Bristol and West, and Woolwich – opened only 105 while shutting down 282. That equals more than one in ten of what was a branch network of 2,583.

> **Branch closures, especially in hard-hit rural areas, also had severe knock-on effects for the local economy**

Last night one of the report's authors, Richard Willis, said the cost of a branch closure was often immeasurable. It left former savers as 'social lepers' forced to travel widely to either get at their money or seek financial advice. Although closures of any financial institution traditionally hit the elderly and infirm, many professionals have also been affected.

'There are teachers and doctors who are terrified of what happens when it comes to sorting out a mortgage for the first time,' said Mr Willis. 'The branch is vital to them and everyone around it.' In 1991, there were 101 building societies in Britain. That number has fallen to 69 and will be further reduced when the Yorkshire-based Bradford and Bingley converts later this year.

'Societies that have converted to plc status are more aggressive in closing branches,' added Mr Willis. 'They become more commercially minded and less socially concerned.' He added that branch closures, especially in hard-hit rural areas, also had severe knock-on effects for the local economy.

'Shops and services may be forced into decline because they are dependent on the close proximity of financial institutions,' he said.

© The Daily Mail
January, 2000

Six rural pubs close each week

Housing boom tightens the squeeze on village inns as pressure grows for rate relief and the development of assistance programmes

Britain's lopsided housing boom is threatening to drive the village pub out of sought-after areas, according to the government's main rural adviser, the Countryside Agency.

Scores of country pubs have been converted into commuter housing or second homes in the past two years, and the rate of closure and sale for housing has now topped six pubs a week, according to research by the agency and the BBC1 programme *Countryfile*.

Falling local demand for a snug place to play darts and have a couple of pints has helped to worsen the malaise, particularly in affluent villages where the average idea of a night out is something grander.

'Things have reached the stage where intervention by the planning authorities or business rate concessions are necessary to save the day,' said Mary Owen, community development officer for the Countryside Agency. 'The other way forward is to encourage pubs to diversify by running the village shop, post office or even doctor's surgery, to supplement trade.'

By Martin Wainwright

The agency is pressing the government to cost out in its rural white paper, due in the early spring, the implications of a 50% discount on business rates for village pubs. The concept chimes with current work by Camra, the campaign for real ale, which is finalising a 'viability test' for local planning authorities to use whenever a brewery or other pub owner applies for change-of-use permission to convert to housing. This is already in use by some of the worst-hit rural local authorities, such as East Cambridgeshire, which has seen 11 pubs in four years turned into expensive homes – much as happened to country vicarages when Anglican dioceses retrenched.

'We now require proof that the pub is no longer viable as a business before we will give consent,' said Charlotte Cane of East Cambridgeshire district council. Landlords have to show that typical ways of developing a pub, including provision of food and children's playgrounds, would not work.

Paul Ainsworth of Camra said: 'A village without a pub is like a village without a heart – if the pub dies, a large part of the village dies as well.'

The campaign has encouraged diversification and local co-operative buyouts – as at Hesket Newmarket in Cumbria, and Reach in Cambridgeshire, both localities with affluent and commercially experienced incomers who have helped such rescues to succeed.

The Countryside Agency is also promoting pub-based enterprise through its village shops scheme in Devon, an area targeted by second-home buyers, where the original idea of rescuing faltering shops now embraces pubs as well.

Ms Owen said: 'This could solve both problems, but 50% rate relief is the measure which would make the real difference. It would increase income by several thousands of pounds a year, and that would go a long way to retain the village pub.'

© *Guardian Newspapers Limited 2000*

Urban sprawl destroys the quiet countryside

The peace and quiet of the countryside is being shattered as never before, anti-noise campaigners warned yesterday.

More and more lives are being made a misery by loud music, barking dogs, traffic and aircraft noise.

The problem is being made worse by urban sprawl, with England losing an area of rural tranquillity almost the size of Wales since the 1960s because of housing development and road building.

By James Chapman, Science Correspondent

Now three environmental groups are uniting to call for Government action on the day which has been dubbed National Noise Action Day.

Tony Burton, the Council for the Protection of Rural England's assistant director, said: 'Tranquillity and the chance to get away from it all are defining features of rural England.

'As rural tranquillity is shattered and it becomes ever harder to find peace and quiet in the countryside near to towns, so the quality of life of the nation is diminished.'

John Stewart, chairman of the United Kingdom Noise Association, said they hoped to lobby Environment Minister Michael Meacher for a comprehensive noise strategy. Research from the National Society for Clean Air and Environmental Protection, published yesterday, showed that complaints about amplified music and dogs continues to increase.

It also showed that informal solutions, such as mediation, are more effective than resorting to law when tackling noise disputes between neighbours.

Richard Mills, NSCA secretary general, said a National Noise Strategy would 'enable us to work towards a more acceptable noise climate for everyone'.

The three largest areas of rural tranquillity in England are found in north Devon, the Marches of Shropshire and Herefordshire, and the north Pennines.

The report suggests the introduction of a network of 'quiet lanes' in the countryside where walkers and riders have priority, and improved access to peaceful areas from towns and cities by public transport.

The CPRE's report shows the South-East has been worst affected, with 35 per cent of the peaceful countryside area lost to urban sprawl since the 1960s. Within the South-East, Greater London has suffered most (81 per cent), followed by Surrey (58 per cent), Berkshire (45 per cent) and West Sussex (40 per cent).

Next comes the West Midlands with an overall loss of 21 per cent – Staffordshire (30 per cent) and Warwickshire (27 per cent) have been particularly badly hit.

The East Midlands and the South-West are just behind on 20 per cent with the area covered by the former county of Avon (51 per cent), Nottinghamshire (43 per cent) and Northamptonshire (31 per cent) the biggest losers in these areas.

Then comes Yorkshire and Humberside and the North-West (both 18 per cent) with Cheshire (35 per cent) and South Yorkshire (48 per cent) among counties worst hit.

East Anglia (11 per cent) and the North-East (9 per cent) have fared best, although Cleveland has lost 44 per cent of its peaceful countryside.

© The Daily Mail
June, 2000

Valuing the sound of silence

National Noise Action Day Rural Tranquillity

Finding peace and quiet in the countryside risks becoming a distant memory across much of England without firm Government action to value and protect rural tranquillity.'

This is the message from CPRE on National Noise Action Day (Wednesday 7 June) as part of a campaign to gain official recognition for tranquillity in the Government's forthcoming Rural White Paper.

England has lost an area of rural tranquillity almost the size of Wales to the impact of rising traffic levels and sprawling development since the 1960s.

Tony Burton, CPRE's Assistant Director, said: 'Tranquillity and the chance to get away from it all are defining features of rural England. As rural tranquillity is shattered and it becomes ever harder to find peace and quiet in the countryside near to towns, so the quality of life of the nation is diminished.

'Time and time again the Government and other official bodies recognise the importance of rural tranquillity but too little is being done to value and protect it.'

CPRE is calling for:
- rural tranquillity to be included as a headline indicator of the quality of life in the Government's forthcoming Rural White Paper;
- local councils to identify tranquil areas and protect them from the impact of built development and rising traffic levels;
- the introduction of a network of Quiet Lanes in the countryside where walkers and riders have priority;
- improved access to tranquil areas from towns and cities by public transport.

Tony Burton concluded: 'The benefits of rural tranquillity should be for the many and not the few. Tranquillity should be available to everyone, and more needs to be done to value and protect it.'

• The above information is from the Council for the Protection of Rural England (CPRE) web site which can be found at www.greenchannel.com/cpre/main.htm

Alternatively, see page 41 for their address details.

© Council for the Protection of
Rural England (CPRE)

My ruined village

The cottages are occupied by bankers and media high fliers. The school has been closed down. The last farmer is on income support. John Mortimer condemns modern life in rural Britain

It is the habit of governments, when they want to interfere in any field of activity, to start by rubbishing those who live through its problems every day. When they want to mould education to their particular purposes they start by letting it be known that all school teachers are ill-disciplined relics of the Sixties. When they plan to do something really outrageous, like denying the right to trial by jury, they denounce lawyers, who might protest, as money-grubbing conservatives. And when they decide to take the giant step of not doing much at all about the plight of rural England, farmers and country dwellers have become hopeless whingers who ought to thank their lucky stars they're not living in Manchester.

I've lived in this village at the edge of the Chilterns for 70 years. When I was a child, we had, within a mile, three pubs, three shops, a post office, two schools, two churches and a chapel. A bus came and took people to the town six miles away and brought them back. Now we have no shops, no post office, no bus. One of the pubs has vanished and another is about to be closed and sold off as a desirable residence to a commuter. Cottages which once contained wood cutters, chair-leg turners and farm workers now change hands at nearly £1 million to house merchant bankers and couples in television. There are few affordable houses for the descendants of the chair-leg turners and farm labourers. One of the churches and the chapel have been converted into expensive homes and, worst of all, there is no school, and when the school goes the heart goes out of a village.

But down a bumpy road, through the beech trees, in a secret and silent valley, we have a local farmer who keeps sheep and cattle. He has a wife and four young children, a radio but no television. His accounts show that, after the deduction of his necessary expenses, he is left with a profit of £9 a week to keep himself and his family. He gets income support so that, presumably, he is perfectly all right. If he talks about the crisis in the countryside, Tony Blair apparently feels justified in asking: 'What crisis?'

> *I've lived in this village at the edge of the Chilterns for 70 years. When I was a child, we had, within a mile, three pubs, three shops, a post office, two schools, two churches and a chapel*

After years of neglect and the mishandling of the BSE crisis by the last government, the farmers and country dwellers were bursting to vote Labour. Their present mood can be judged by the huge, well-behaved countryside marches and the reception given to bland government Ministers pointing out, with singular ineptitude, various alternatives to farming.

Our local sheep farmer should, they say, start a riding school, but he's no horseman and has no money to buy horses. He should open a theme park, but neither he nor the Government have much of a talent for theme parks. He should take in bed and breakfast visitors, but his family occupy all the bedrooms. The Government's solutions can only remind you of the one-legged actor in Peter Cook's sketch who has it in mind to play Tarzan.

The truth of the matter is that the Government is standing back and allowing farming to die, just as Mrs Thatcher presided over the death throes of heavy industry. Twenty-two thousand farmers went out of business last year, and another 22,000 the year before. There's £360m waiting in Brussels to compensate farmers for the strong pound, but the Government won't take it because they would have to provide matching money – only half the sum blown on the transient Dome. Farmers, some hundreds of whom have been driven to suicide, now have to watch another £60m being handed out to a 'millennium experience' utterly remote from the England of Cumbrian hillsides and Devon villages.

If England is thought of with affection it's often because of our countryside. Our literature, from Chaucer to Shakespeare, Milton, Wordsworth, Emily Brontë and D.H. Lawrence, is seasoned in the country, the fields and woodlands. It's the business of government to see that it's preserved for the pleasure and sanity of all of us. The fatal mistake has been to imagine that the interests of the countryside are in some way different from the interests of farmers. The countryside can only be maintained by a healthy agriculture. If farming dies a most precious part of England dies with it.

We're told, on the basis of doubtful and speculative statistics, that 3.8 million new houses are needed to cover our green and pleasant land, 900,000 in South-East England. Such houses, if needed, should be used to reclaim inner cities. We might have suggested they should be used to give jobs and provide benefits in the neglected North, did we not have it on Tony Blair's good authority that the North-South divide is as imaginary as the crisis in the countryside.

The fox-hunting issue, which raises so much political excitement, is an example of the suspicion by urbanised MPs that the country is the home of bloodthirsty toffs.

Hunting, far easier to defend than shooting or fishing, is enjoyed by many country dwellers including unemployed Welsh miners, long-distance lorry drivers and the mounted police. The Bill, proposed by Mr Foster and voted for enthusiastically by Labour MPs, would have made it a criminal offence to walk a dog which started to chase a rabbit and then changed its mind and ran after a hare. When an MP had to admit to Jeremy Paxman that he couldn't tell a rabbit from a hare, those in the country who regard hunting as a reasonable and legitimate pursuit were left wondering at the depths of our legislators' ignorance. It seems to us an acceptable way of controlling foxes which, having no concern for animal rights, slaughter our chickens and lambs.

We are also left wondering at a government which wants to raise road taxes and petrol prices when life in the country would mean permanent house arrest without a motor car. We are disturbed by the social divisions between town and country caused by criminalising hunters.

We wonder at the hostility of a government which was genuinely welcomed by many voters in marginal country seats. We were astonished when a party in Downing Street, intended to welcome country representatives, excluded the Countryside Alliance and the Society for the Preservation of Rural England, which is like having a party for theatricals and failing to invite anyone from the Royal Shakespeare Company or the National Theatre.

Above all, we feel that the English countryside, and a healthy agriculture, would be a more lasting tribute to the millennium than a voyage inside a plastic human body on a remote site in Greenwich.

© Guardian Newspapers Limited 2000

Not so Merrie England

Poverty and its related problems are rife in areas facilely considered as rural idylls, says Derek Brown

The charms of the English countryside mask a host of social ills, highlighted by the Countryside Agency in its latest report.

Three million rural dwellers live below the official poverty line of half the average national income. In Cornwall, thought by many to be the most idyllic of English counties, average wages are less than three-quarters of the national norm.

Ewen Cameron, Agency chairman and West Country landowner, had some hard home truths for a London conference on social exclusion in the countryside.

'Some people in rural areas face disadvantage as acute as those in urban areas: low income, lack of a secure home, difficulties reaching health care and services, social isolation, and powerlessness. The difference is they are often hidden; obscured in the wider community alongside people in very different circumstances.'

Cameron's comments go to the heart of a rapidly growing social gap, as serious as the so-called north-south divide or the national gap between rich and poor.

That is, the gulf of incomes and opportunities between the rural affluent and the rural deprived. The polarisation is accelerating as wealthy people move to parts of the countryside where farm incomes are falling, and unemployment remains stubbornly high.

In the Cotswolds, the quintessence of the rural idyll and the full- or part-time home of many rich newcomers, 27% of households have annual incomes of less than £7,000.

In a Wiltshire village surveyed by the Countryside Agency, a third of households had incomes below £6,000, while another third had more than £40,000.

The rural divide, however, goes deeper than crude incomes. As more and more urban dwellers head for the delights of country life, house prices are rising relentlessly – especially in the counties within striking distance of London.

Earlier this year, the agency estimated that up to 10,000 new affordable homes were needed each year to meet the needs of the rural population. But in the seven years to 1997, a total of just 18,000 were built.

As more and more urban dwellers head for the delights of country life, house prices are rising relentlessly

---

As many as one in six of young adults born in rural communities are leaving for the cities because they can no longer afford to live in the country. And those who stay face a grim task finding work.

Unemployment figures for rural areas are often grotesquely distorted: by the influx of retired newcomers, the inclusion of country-dwellers who commute to work in towns, and by the relatively large proportion of part-time and seasonal jobs.

Income levels are more transparent. Average weekly wages in Cornwall, for example, are £297, in Northumberland £315, and in the Isle of Wight £323. That compares with a national average of £405.

More telling than any number of raw statistics, however, are the comments from case studies featured in the agency's latest report. One farming couple in the Peak District, somehow living on a quarter of the national minimum wage, comment: 'When we got this farm it was a dream come true. But it's a nightmare now.'

A farm worker who has been without work for nine years tells how 'the bottom dropped out of our world'. And an 18-year-old Cornish youth, both jobless and homeless, poignantly records: 'Life was great until I hit 12.'

© Guardian Newspapers Limited 2000

ADDITIONAL RESOURCES

You might like to contact the following organisations for further information. Due to the increasing cost of postage, many organisations cannot respond to enquiries unless they receive a stamped, addressed envelope.

Campaign for the Protection of Rural Wales (CPRW)
Ty Gwyn
31 High Street
Welshpool, Powys, SY21 7YD
Tel: 01938 552525
Fax: 01938 552741
E-mail: info@cprw.org.uk
Web site: www.cprw.org.uk
Works to protect the Welsh countryside and coast. Encourages sustainable rural development.

Council for the Protection of Rural England (CPRE)
Warwick House
25 Buckingham Palace Road
London, SW1W 0PP
Tel: 020 7976 6433
Fax: 020 7976 6373
E-mail: info@cpre.org.uk
Web site: www.greenchannel.com/cpre
CPRE is a national charity which helps people to protect the countryside where there is threat, to enhance it where there is opportunity, and to keep it beautiful, productive and enjoyable for everyone.

Countryside Agency
Environmental Protection Unit
John Dower House
Crescent Place
Cheltenham, GL50 3RA
Tel: 01242 521381
Fax: 01242 584270
E-mail: info@countryside.gov.uk
Web site: www.countryside.gov.uk
The Countryside Agency is the new statutory body working to conserve and enhance the countryside.

Friends of the Earth (FOE)
26-28 Underwood Street
London, N1 7JQ
Tel: 020 7490 1555
Fax: 020 7490 0881
E-mail: info@foe.co.uk
Web site: www.foe.co.uk
As an independent environmental group, Friends of the Earth publishes a comprehensive range of leaflets, books and in-depth briefings and reports.

Green Party of England and Wales
1a Waterlow Road
Archway
London, N19 5NJ
Tel: 020 7272 4474
Fax: 020 7272 6653
E-mail: gptyoffice@gn.apc.org
Web site: www.greenparty.org.uk
The Green Party believes that humankind is especially responsible for the care of the planet, holding it in trust for all other living things and for future generations.

National Farmers' Union (NFU)
164 Shaftesbury Avenue
London, WC2H 8HL
Tel: 020 7331 7200
Fax: 020 7331 7313
E-mail: nfu@nfu.org.uk
Web site: www.nfu.org.uk
The National Farmers' Union is the democratic organisation representing farmers and growers in England and Wales. Its central objective is to promote the interests of those farming businesses producing high quality food and drink products for customers and markets, both at home and abroad.

National Housing Federation (NHF)
175 Gray's Inn Road
London, WC1X 8UP
Tel: 020 7278 6571
Fax: 020 7833 8323
E-mail: info@housing.org.uk
Web site: www.housing.org.uk
The National Housing Federation is the body that represents the independent social housing sector.

The Ramblers' Association
2nd Floor, Camelford House
87-90 Albert Embankment
London, SE1 7TW
Tel: 020 7339 8500
Fax: 020 7339 8501
E-mail: ramblers@london.ramblers.org.uk
Web site: www.ramblers.org.uk
Promotes rambling, protects rights of way, campaigns for access to open country and defends the beauty of the countryside. Produces publications.

Sustain
94 White Lion Street
London, N1 9PF
Tel: 020 7837 1228
Fax: 020 7837 1141
E-mail: safe@gn.apc.org
Web site: www.gn.apc.org/safe
Sustain is the alliance for better food and agriculture policies and practices that enhance the health and welfare of people and animals, improve the working and living environment, enrich society and culture and promote equity.

The Wildlife Trust
UK Operation Centre
The Kiln, Waterside
Mather Road
Newark, NG24 1WT
Tel: 01636 677711
Fax: 01636 670001
E-mail: info@wildlife-trust.cix.co.uk
Web site: www.wildlifetrust.org.uk
Has a nationwide network of local trusts working to protect wildlife in town and country.

INDEX

```
┌──────────────────────────────────────────────────────────────┐
│ ■ ▬▬▬▬▬▬▬▬▬▬▬▬  Independence Web News  ▬▬▬▬▬▬▬▬▬▬▬▬  ⊡▤ │
├──────────────────────────────────────────────────────────────┤
│ ⇐o    o⇒    🏠      Ⓡ     📷      ⇒°    🖨     🔍      ⬤        │
│ Back Forward Home  Reload Images  Open  Print  Find    Stop    │
├──────────────────────────────────────────────────────────────┤
│ [                                                            ] │
├──────────────────────────────────────────────────────────────┤
│ [Live Home Page]  [Search]  [Computer]  [Support]  [System]    │
└──────────────────────────────────────────────────────────────┘
```

★★★★★

The Internet has been likened to shopping in a supermarket without aisles. The press of a button on a Web browser can bring up thousands of sites but working your way through them to find what you want can involve long and frustrating on-line searches. And unfortunately many sites contain inaccurate, misleading or heavily biased information. Our researchers have therefore undertaken an extensive analysis to bring you a selection of quality Web site addresses.

Council for the Protection of Rural England (CPRE)
www.cpre.org.uk
CPRE seeks to provide well-researched, intelligent and practical solutions to problems which affect the English countryside. A useful web site which has the following information: press releases, publications, catalogue, policy resources, volunteer opportunities.

Friends of the Earth (FOE)
www.foe.co.uk
By clicking on National Campaigns followed by Atmosphere and Transport you will find information and press releases on FOEs housing campaign including halting greenfield housing and protecting the environment.

Countryside Agency
www.countryside.gov.uk
The State of the Countryside 2000. This report for England gives a concise and informative overview of facts and trends about England's rural areas. It is an important reference tool for anyone with an interest in the countryside, including policy makers, researchers and the media. You can download the full PDF file (1.7 MB).

House Builders' Federation
www.hbf.co.uk
The House Builders Federation is the voice of the house building industry in England and Wales. Click on Current Issues for a range of press releases and reports on housing issues.

ACKNOWLEDGEMENTS

The publisher is grateful for permission to reproduce the following material.

While every care has been taken to trace and acknowledge copyright, the publisher tenders its apology for any accidental infringement or where copyright has proved untraceable. The publisher would be pleased to come to a suitable arrangement in any such case with the rightful owner.

Chapter One: Urban Trends

Britain's housing problem explained, © Guardian Newspapers Limited, 2000, *Town grouse and country grouse,* © Guardian Newspapers Limited, 2000, *Urban footprints,* © Council for the Protection of Rural England (CPRE), *Room to live,* © Council for the Protection of Rural England (CPRE), *Housing people and the environment,* © National Housing Federation, *Plans and planning,* © The Wildlife Trust, *Waiting for Lord Rogers's urban renaissance,* © The Economist Newspaper Limited, London, 5th August 2000, *Leaving,* © Office for National Statistics (ONS), *Urban anxieties,* © Crown copyright material is reproduced with the permission of the Controller of Her Majesty's Stationery Office, *Building and urban development,* © IPC Media Ltd, *Halt greenfield housing,* © Friends of the Earth, *What's behind the 4.4 million extra households?,* © Green Party of England and Wales, *Cry the beloved countryside,* © IPC Media Ltd, *How to campaign on supermarket developments,* © Sustain, *Fighting urban sprawl,* © Friends of the Earth, *City rich prop up rural poor,* © Guardian Newspapers Limited, 2000, July 1999.

Chapter Two: Impact on the Countryside

The housing crisis is not just an urban phenomenon, © Guardian Newspapers Limited, 2000, *The rural revolution,* © The Daily Mail, October 1999, *People and houses and the countryside,* © Council for the Protection of Rural Wales (CPRW), *Coastline of sand and cement,* © National Farmers' Union (NFU), *Meacher announces better protection for countryside,* © Ramblers' Association, *Developers getting the green message,* © The Countryside Agency, *The state of the countryside 2000,* © The Countryside Agency, *Rural problems,* © Guardian Newspapers Limited, 2000, *Land under threat and protection,* © National Farmers' Union (NFU), *Loophole threatens our village greens,* © The Independent, May 2000, *Villages suffering as new banks close scores of branches,* © The Daily Mail, January 2000, *Six rural pubs close each week,* © Guardian Newspapers Limited, 2000, *Urban sprawl destroys the quiet countryside,* © The Daily Mail, June 2000, *Valuing the sound of silence,* © Council for the Protection of Rural England (CPRE), *My ruined village,* © Guardian Newspapers Limited, 2000, *Not so Merrie England,* © Guardian Newspapers Limited, 2000.

Photographs and illustrations:

Pages 1, 4, 13, 18, 25, 29, 35: Pumpkin House, pages 3, 8, 14, 20, 23, 26, 32, 36: Simon Kneebone.

Craig Donnellan
Cambridge
September, 2000